COMPUTERS, INTERNET, AND SOCIETY

Computers in Science and Mathematics

COMPUTERS, INTERNET, AND SOCIETY

Computers in Science and Mathematics

Robert Plotkin

Facts On File
An Infobase Learning Company

COMPUTERS IN SCIENCE AND MATHEMATICS

Facts On File, Inc.
An imprint of Infobase Learning
132 West 31st Street
New York NY 10001

Library of Congress Cataloging-in-Publication Data

Plotkin, Robert, 1971–
    Computers in science and mathematics / Robert Plotkin.
        p. cm. — (Computers, internet, and society)
    Includes bibliographical references and index.
    ISBN 978-0-8160-7757-1 (alk. paper)
    1. Science—Data processing. 2. Mathematics—Data processing. 3. Computers—History. I. Title.
    Q183.9.P56 2011
    502.85—dc22   2010047046

Facts On File books are available at special discounts when purchased in bulk quantities for businesses, associations, institutions, or sales promotions. Please call our Special Sales Department in New York at (212) 967-8800 or (800) 322-8755.

You can find Facts On File on the World Wide Web at http://www.infobaselearning.com

Text design by Kerry Casey
Composition by Hermitage Publishing Services
Illustrations by Bobbi McCutcheon
Photo research by Suzanne M. Tibor
Cover printed by Bang Printing, Brainerd, Minn.
Book printed and bound by Bang Printing, Brainerd, Minn.
Date printed: October 2011
Printed in the United States of America

10 9 8 7 6 5 4 3 2 1

CONTENTS

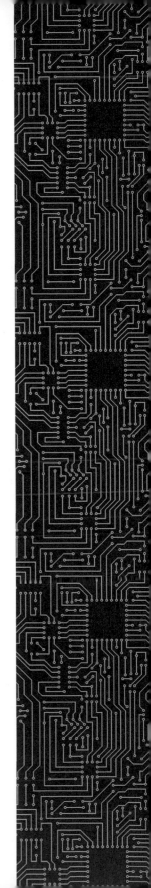

PREFACE

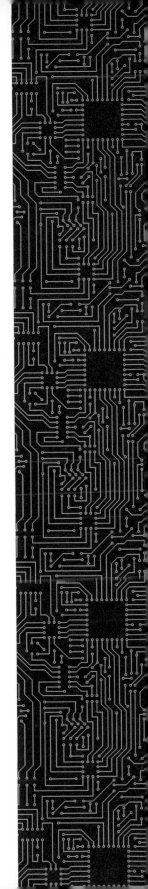

Computers permeate innumerable aspects of people's lives. For example, computers are used to communicate with friends and family, analyze finances, play games, watch movies, listen to music, purchase products and services, and learn about the world. People increasingly use computers without even knowing it, as microprocessors containing software replace mechanical and electrical components in everything from automobiles to microwave ovens to wristwatches.

Conversations about computers tend to focus on their technological features, such as how many billions of calculations they can perform per second, how much memory they contain, or how small they have become. We have good reason to be amazed at advances in computer technology over the last 50 years. According to one common formulation of Moore's law (named after Gordon Moore of Intel Corporation), the number of transistors on a chip doubles roughly every two years. As a result, a computer that can be bought for $1,000 today is as powerful as a computer that cost more than $1 million just 15 years ago.

Although such technological wonders are impressive in their own right, we care about them not because of the engineering achievements they represent but because they have changed how people interact every day. E-mail not only enables communication with existing friends and family more quickly and less expensively but also lets us forge friendships with strangers halfway across the globe. Social networking platforms such as Twitter and Facebook enable nearly instant, effortless communication among large groups of people without requiring the time or effort needed to compose and read e-mail messages. These and other forms of communication are facilitated by increasingly powerful mobile handheld devices, such as the BlackBerry and iPhone, which make it possible for people to communicate at any time and in any place, thereby eliminating the need for a desktop computer with a hardwired Internet connection. Such improvements in technology have led to changes in society, often in complex and unexpected ways.

Understanding the full impact that computers have on society therefore requires an appreciation of not only what computers can do but also how computer technology is used in practice and its effects on human behavior and attitudes.

Computers, Internet, and Society is a timely multivolume set that seeks to provide students with such an understanding. The set includes the following six titles, each of which focuses on a particular context in which computers have a significant social impact:

- *Communication and Cyberspace*
- *Computer Ethics*
- *Computers and Creativity*
- *Computers in Science and Mathematics*
- *Computers in the Workplace*
- *Privacy, Security, and Cyberspace*

It is the goal of each volume to accomplish the following:

- explain the history of the relevant computer technology, what such technology can do today, and how it works;
- explain how computers interact with human behavior in a particular social context; and
- encourage readers to develop socially responsible attitudes and behaviors in their roles as computer users and future developers of computer technology.

New technology can be so engrossing that people often adopt it—and adapt their behavior to it—quickly and without much forethought. Yesterday's students gathered in the schoolyard to plan for a weekend party; today they meet online on a social networking Web site. People flock to such new features as soon as they come available, as evidenced by the long lines at the store every time a newer, smarter phone is announced.

Most such developments are positive. Yet they also carry implications for our privacy, freedom of speech, and security, all of which are easily overlooked if one does not pause to think about them. The paradox of today's computer technology is that it is both everywhere and invisible. The goal of this set is to make such technology visible so that it, and its impact on society, can be examined, as well as to assist students in using conceptual tools for making informed and responsible decisions about how to both apply and further develop that technology now and as adults.

Although today's students are more computer savvy than all of the generations that preceded them, many students are more familiar with what computers can do than with how computers work or the social changes being wrought by computers. Students who use the Internet constantly may remain unaware of how computers can be used to invade their privacy or steal their identity or how journalists and human rights activists use computer encryption technology to keep their communications secret and secure from oppressive governments around the world. Students who have grown up copying information from the World Wide Web and downloading songs, videos, and feature-length films onto computers, iPods, and cell phones may not understand the circumstances under which those activities are legitimate and when they violate copyright law. And students who have only learned about scientists and inventors in history books probably are unaware that today's innovators are using computers to discover new drugs and write pop music at the touch of a button.

In fact, young people have had such close and ongoing interactions with computers since they were born that they often lack the historical perspective to understand just how much computers have made their lives different from those of their parents. Computers form as much of the background of students' lives as the air they breathe; as a result, they tend to take both for granted. This set, therefore, is highly relevant and important to students because it enables them to understand not only how computers work but also how computer technology has affected their lives. The goal of this set is to provide students with the intellectual tools needed to think critically about computer technology so that they can make informed and responsible decisions about how to both use and further develop that technology now and as adults.

This set reflects my long-standing personal and professional interest in the intersection between computer technology, law, and society. I started programming computers when I was about 10 years old and my fascination with the technology has endured ever since. I had the honor of studying computer science and engineering at the Massachusetts Institute of Technology (MIT) and then studying law at the Boston University School of Law, where I now teach a course entitled, "Software and the Law." Although I spend most of my time as a practicing patent lawyer, focusing on patent protection for computer technology, I have also spoken and written internationally on topics including patent protection for software, freedom of speech, electronic privacy, and ethical implications of releasing potentially harmful software. My book, *The Genie in the Machine,* explores the impact of computer-automated inventing on law, businesses, inventors, and consumers.

What has been most interesting to me has been to study not any one aspect of computer technology, but rather to delve into the wide range of ways in which such technology affects, and is affected by, society. As a result, a multidisciplinary set such as this is a perfect fit for my background and interests. Although it can be challenging to educate non-technologists about how computers work, I have written and spoken about such topics to audiences including practicing lawyers, law professors, computer scientists and engineers, ethicists, philosophers, and historians. Even the work that I have targeted solely to lawyers has been multidisciplinary in nature, drawing on the history and philosophy of computer technology to provide context and inform my legal analysis. I specifically designed my course on "Software and the Law" to be understandable to law students with no background in computer technology. I have leveraged this experience in explaining complex technical concepts to lay audiences in the writing of this multidisciplinary set for a student audience in a manner that is understandable and engaging to students of any background.

The world of computers changes so rapidly that it can be difficult even for those of us who spend most of our waking hours learning about the latest developments in computer technology to stay up to date. The term *technological singularity* has even been coined to refer to a point, perhaps not too far in the future, when the rate of technological change will become so rapid that essentially no time elapses between one technological advance and the next. For better or worse, time does elapse between writing a series of books such as this and the date of publication. With full awareness of the need to provide students with current and relevant information, every effort has been made, up to the time at which these volumes are shipped to the printers, to ensure that each title in this set is as up to date as possible.

ACKNOWLEDGMENTS

Many people deserve thanks for making this series a reality. First, my thanks to my literary agent, Jodie Rhodes, for introducing me to Facts On File. When she first approached me, it was to ask whether I knew any authors who were interested in writing a set of books on a topic that I know nothing about—I believe it was biology. In response, I asked whether there might be interest in a topic closer to my heart—computers and society—and, as they say, the rest is history.

Frank Darmstadt, my editor, has not only held my hand through all of the high-level planning and low-level details involved in writing a series of this magnitude but also exhibited near superhuman patience in the face of drafts whose separation in time could be marked by the passing of the seasons. He also helped me to toe the fine dividing line between the forest and the trees and between today's technological marvels and tomorrow's long-forgotten fads—a distinction that is particularly difficult to draw in the face of rapidly changing technology. I also thank Michael Axon for his incisive review of the manuscript and Alexandra Simon for her superb copyediting.

Several research assistants, including Catie Watson, Rebekah Judson, Jessica McElrath, and Sue Keeler, provided invaluable aid in uncovering and summarizing information about technologies ranging from the ancient to the latest gadgets we carry in our pockets. In particular, Luba Jabsky performed extensive research that formed the foundation of many of the book's chapters and biographies.

The artwork and photographs have brought the text to life. Although computer science, with its microscopic electronic components and abstract software modules, is a particularly difficult field to illustrate, line artist Bobbi McCutcheon and photo researcher Suzie Tibor could not have matched visuals to text more perfectly.

Last, but not least, I thank my family, including my partner, Melissa, and my dog, Maggie, for standing by my side and at my feet, respectively, as I spent my evenings and weekends trying, through words and pictures, to convey to the next generation some of the wonder and excitement in computer technology that I felt as a teenager.

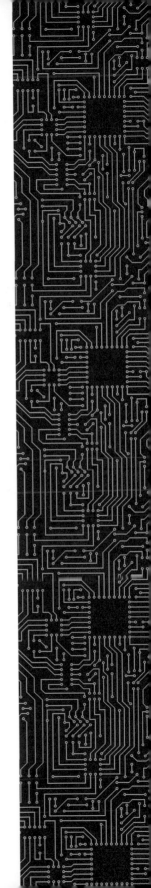

INTRODUCTION

Computers in Science and Mathematics explores both the contributions that scientists and mathematicians have made to computer technology and the varied ways in which scientists and mathematicians use computers in their daily work. Scientists and mathematicians are always seeking new ways to perform increasingly complex calculations more quickly and easily than before so they can solve more difficult problems with less effort. As a result, they have always been at the forefront of inventing tools for performing computations so they could use such tools in their own work. In the modern era, scientists and mathematicians continue to be pivotal in the development of computer hardware and software, in the theory underlying the design of computer systems, and in the use of computers to advance science and mathematics. Science and mathematics as we know them today could hardly continue to advance without computers and their accompanying software. *Computers in Science and Mathematics* provides a history of computers as scientific and mathematical tools followed by many examples of how computers are being used today to solve an increasingly wide range of scientific and mathematical problems.

For example, even before automated calculating machines existed, mathematicians created written number systems to simplify the process of performing calculations. Just try dividing 9,782,118 by 23 using long division without using pencil and paper (or a *calculator* or computer) to understand how important written number systems are for performing calculations. Long before scientists harnessed electricity, *mechanical calculating devices* such as the *abacus,* the Greek Antikythera mechanism, and the Speeding Clock were used to perform computations for use in fields such as astronomy and navigation. Subsequent devices that incorporated numbered keys and that still did not require electricity were used well into the 20th century. The crowning achievement of such mechanical calculators was the *Analytical Engine,* a computer designed in the mid-18th century capable of being programmed to perform any calculation but never built due to its complexity and lack of political and financial support.

In the 20th-century, scientists, mathematicians, and philosophers picked up where their predecessors left off but with the benefit of increased theoretical knowledge of how to perform computations and practical knowledge of how to design smaller, faster electrical circuits for carrying out such computations. The basic theory underlying today's computers, which can be programmed with software to perform nearly any function, was developed in the 1930s. Soon after, pioneers of the computing age began to build increasingly large and powerful calculating devices that could be programmed to perform various calculations without needing to physically rewire the machines' circuitry. By the 1950s, these computers had taken the basic form that they continue to have today, although on a much larger scale—a single computer would take up an entire room. The invention of the transistor and advances in electromagnetic memories, however, soon enabled such mammoths to decrease rapidly in size. The high cost of these machines meant that they were used primarily by governments, large companies, and universities to perform tasks such as compiling accounting records and computing ballistics tables for use in wartime.

One of the first practical successes of modern computers represented a perfect intersection between mathematical theory and engineering practice. *Cryptography* is the science of scrambling messages so they cannot be read if intercepted in transit. *Encryption* is particularly valuable during wartime for keeping messages secret from an enemy. Although in theory an encrypted message can be deciphered by trying all possible ways to descramble it, in practice the number of possibilities is too large to make such a brute force approach to the problem work. As a result, successfully cracking an encryption scheme requires clever use of mathematics to uncover patterns in the coded messages. British mathematicians and engineers achieved such a feat in World War II to crack the code used by the German "Enigma" encryption machine, arguably enabling the war to end several years earlier than it would have otherwise. Modern encryption, which is used to keep everything from financial information to medical records to personal e-mail hidden from prying eyes, continues to draw deeply from its mathematical underpinnings.

Although scientists often use mathematics to design experiments and develop theories and although mathematicians often generalize from the data gathered by scientists to identify mathematical laws of nature, mathematics differs from science in a fundamental way. Knowledge gained from science, no matter how well verified by observation, is never completely certain. The law of gravity might not hold true everywhere in the universe and at all times. Even if it does, it is never possible to know absolutely, because scientists cannot make observations everywhere and at all times. Mathematics, in contrast, can produce knowledge that can be proved to be true without any doubt. Many *mathematical proofs* exist, for example, that demonstrate with complete certainty that the square root of two is an irrational number, meaning that it cannot be written as a ratio of two integers, such as ¾, or as a decimal number that terminates (such as 0.75) or that repeats the same sequence indefinitely (such as ⅓, which can be written as 0.333, with the 3s repeating indefinitely). Although throughout most of history mathematical proofs were created by mathematicians who followed rules of logic, in recent years, computers have been used to generate proofs to solve some of mathematics' thorniest problems. The use of computers to prove mathematical truths is raising new questions about the meaning of truth and its relationship to mathematics and to mathematicians.

Although scientists strive to find truths that are as general as possible, they are limited to doing so by observing the natural world. Scientists use the scientific method to form a hypothesis—such as the principle that opposite poles of a magnet attract each other—and then conduct experiments in the real world to test the hypothesis, such as by placing different poles of magnets next to each other and observing which ones attract and which ones repel each other. Without the ability to conduct such experiments, scientific hypotheses could never be verified, would remain little more than speculation, and would be of no more value than science fiction. However, computers are now making it possible to simulate aspects of the real world ranging from the motion of solid particles through fluids to the spread of fires to the effects of disease on animal and human populations. With such *simulators* at hand, both scientists and engineers can conduct simulated experiments *in virtual worlds* and, so long as the simulators are accurate enough, draw conclusions about the real world without having to observe it directly. Although most people are familiar with simulators from their use in creating realistic characters, vehicles, and weapons in videogames, simulators are being used today by scientists to make real and groundbreaking scientific discoveries.

One of the most widespread uses of simulators is for use in predicting short-term weather events and long-term climate changes. For most of human history, weather prediction was more of an art than a science and one that was often fraught with superstition and methods lacking any scientific basis. Even reliable techniques often could not be used to predict the weather more than a few hours into the future. The science of weather prediction has changed radically in the last half century as a result of the use of computers to predict weather using simulators that take into account not only vast quantities of historical weather data but also a constant real-time feed of local, regional, and even international data about temperature, pressure, wind speeds, ocean currents, and other conditions. Such simulators combine such data with the latest scientific understanding about how weather patterns develop to simulate the paths the weather will take in the future. Although the complex nature of weather systems imposes fundamental limits on the ability of even the most powerful computers to predict the weather more than a few days into the future, advances in computer-based weather prediction now routinely make it possible to predict devastating events such as hurricanes, tornadoes, tsunamis, and even earthquakes in enough time to give warning to affected populations and save countless lives.

Although humans first designed computers only about 50 years ago, at around the same time, biologists discovered that the natural world contains a mechanism for performing something analogous to computations using a natural biological material: DNA, sometimes called "the code of life." Every cell of every living being contains a complete copy of that organism's DNA, which includes the complete instructions for constructing the entire organism. In this sense, DNA is like a computer that contains software that can be run to grow a plant or animal. Although biologists at first studied DNA to understand how it works in its natural state, more recently biologists, computer scientists, and engineers have been taking advantage of the analogy between DNA and computers to modify DNA, effectively programming it like a computer to perform computations. Although this field of "*DNA computing*" is still in its infancy, some believe it holds the promise of creating biological computers that could outperform today's electronic computers by thousands or millions of times. Many, however, are raising ethical questions about exploiting the fundamental building block of life for use as a computing machine.

Conversely and less controversially, computer scientists are drawing on what biologists have learned about immune systems, brains, natural selection, and other biological phenomena to design computer hardware and software that function more like the natural world than traditional computers. *Artificial neural networks* "learn" to solve problems in a way that mimics the human brain.

Network security software uses *artificial immune systems* to ward off and eliminate intruding computer viruses. *Evolutionary computation* software "evolves" aerodynamic designs for airplane wings in a way that mimics how species of plants and animals evolve to be fit for survival in their natural environments. As computer scientists incorporate features of the biological world into computer systems, they enable computers to heal themselves, learn from their mistakes, and even develop new abilities. Some of these systems are being used to conduct complete scientific experiments and thereby discover new scientific truths. *Computers in Science and Mathematics* explores all of these and additional ways in which scientists and mathematicians are creating new computer systems and using those systems to advance our understanding of the natural and artificial worlds we inhabit.

Chapter 1 traces the evolution of counting devices, beginning with prehistoric tally sticks discovered by archaeologists, including the widely used abacus device. The chapter also describes the earliest use of symbols to represent numbers and the development of number systems by the ancient Babylonians, Egyptians, and Romans. The Arabic number system, the basis for our current decimal number system, is also discussed. Then the focus moves to calculators and other devices that perform mathematical functions. The earliest known calculator, the Antikythera Mechanism, is described, along with several other early calculators. One of the most notable is the *Pascaline,* invented by the mathematician Blaise Pascal in 1642, which was capable of performing calculations using rotating dials. The Industrial Revolution led to a demand for better calculating machines. Charles Babbage was one of the inventors who responded to this demand in 1821 with the design of the Difference Engine, the first automatic calculating engine, and the Analytical Engine, the prototype for modern programmable computers. Chapter 1 concludes with a description of Babbage's groundbreaking designs.

Chapter 2 explores the development of computers in the 20th century. During World War II, mathematicians in England and the United States devised sophisticated machines to decode secret German communications. This chapter describes the *Bombe,* the most famous decoding machine, designed by two mathematicians from Cambridge University, Alan Turing and Gordon Welchman. Turing is now recognized as one of the founders of the field of computer science for his later research into computer design theory and his design of one of the first computers. This chapter also describes the development of early large-scale digital computers, including the *Harvard Mark I,* the *ENIAC,* and the *EDVAC.* These computers used tens of thousands of fragile *vacuum tubes* and weighed several tons. This chapter tracks advances in computer hardware technology, from transistors in the 1950s to *integrated circuits* in the 1960s. The miniaturization of electronic circuitry on silicon *chips* enabled the development of personal computers and other "smart" electronic devices that are now part of everyday life.

Chapter 3 focuses on the history and science of cryptography. The desire to send secret messages has its roots in the origins of written communication. The process of scrambling a message for secrecy and then descrambling it to reveal its meaning is known as encryption (or encoding) and *decryption* (or decoding). Cryptology is the field that formally studies encryption and decryption. The previous chapter described the role that early computing devices played in encrypting and decrypting top secret messages during World War II. This chapter explains how simple encryption schemes work, including a famous scheme called the Caesar shift cipher developed by the ancient Romans. This cipher performed encryption and decryption using a formula known as a key. When encrypted messages are based on a key that is known to both the sender and receiver, there is a danger that messages will be intercepted and decoded by someone who knows the key or figures it out. Solutions for this problem led to sophisticated schemes that use *public keys, digital signatures,* and certificates. This chapter explains the importance of these schemes in everyday life. Sensitive data that travel across computer networks, including passwords, financial transactions, medical information, and even e-mail, are kept secure thanks to public keys and digital signatures. Chapter 3 concludes with a look at *RSA encryption,* currently the most widely used cryptography system.

Chapter 4 explores the use of computers for mathematical proofs, which are formal demonstrations that use a set of established rules to show that a conclusion (or *theorem*) is true. Several types of mathematical proofs are briefly described in this chapter, and one specific proof (that the square root of 2 is an irrational number) is covered in detail. An important component of a *mathematical proof* is to show beyond doubt that a mathematical statement is true for all cases; this must be done without requiring each case to be proved separately. Due to the potentially large number of steps involved, complex mathematical proofs are a perfect application for computers. Mathematicians can write computer software that will exhaustively perform the calculations needed for each case of a proof. This type of *computer-assisted proof* is not without controversy. Some mathematicians claim proofs that involve a large number of computer calculations are difficult or impossible for a human to verify. This chapter examines the arguments for and against the validity of computer-assisted proofs. It also describes how in 1976 the *"four-color theorem"* became the first major theorem to be proven using a computer-assisted proof.

Chapter 5 examines simulators, which are devices or software that create a virtual version of reality. One of the most widely used software simulators is the Microsoft *Flight Simulator,* which is used both for entertainment and as a training aid for pilots. The benefits of simulators for training are described, including cost savings and increased safety and control. In addition to flight training, simulators are used in medical and military training. This chapter then explores the use of simulators as forms of entertainment. Today's realistic 3D video games are a form of simulation. The game represents a virtual world inhabited by fictional characters as well as by *avatars* that represent game players. Some of the most popular simulation games are described as well as simulators such as Second Life, which allow participants to create an alternative life in a virtual world. The chapter then moves to the use of computer simulators in the sciences, where they are used in scientific experiments, social science *modeling,* and engineering design.

Chapter 6 looks at weather tracking and forecasting. Weather forecasting was important for agriculture and navigation in ancient cultures and has continued to be important throughout history. Early methods for predicting weather were often based on superstition and folklore. Over time, logical methods based on the observance of previous weather patterns were employed. The importance of almanacs as sources for weather information is discussed. Early devices that aided in weather predictions are also described in this chapter as well as the role of the telegraph in collating and transmitting weather data. The chapter then focuses on the role computers have played in modern weather prediction. Computer models now allow meteorologists to predict weather with some certainty one week into the future and to predict weather trends months in advance. Computers are also used for *climate models* that study how the world's climate will respond to various global climate changes. Chapter 6 also describes the use of weather satellites and weather radar.

Chapter 7 examines one of the new frontiers of computer technology. The history of computers has been dominated by electronic devices, but researchers are now finding that devices based on biology are also viable. This chapter explains how nanotechnology and bioengineering use individual molecules and organic matter in place of integrated circuitry and silicon chips. The genetic substance known as DNA plays an important role in the field of bioengineering. The discovery of DNA by James Watson and Francis Crick is described along with the structure and function of the substance. Research into DNA computing is explained in this chapter, and an example is presented of how it has been used to solve the "*traveling salesman problem,*" a classic problem in the field of computer science. The groundbreaking work of Leonard Adleman and other scientists is also described. The chapter concludes with a description of the benefits and potential future uses of DNA computing, which promises to offer increased performance and greater energy efficiency compared to electronic computing. However, widespread use of DNA in computing is still in the theoretical stages. The challenges facing this new branch of computer science are also presented in this chapter.

Chapter 8 continues the exploration of computing frontiers that began in chapter 7. Despite the impressive advances that have occurred in computer technology over the previous few decades, there are some severe limitations in current computer technology. Many complex calculations that involve massive amounts of data are not feasible using current technology. The fundamental architecture of today's computers, which is based on the execution of one step at a time, is not compatible with processes that involve simultaneous events (such as stock trading). Other limitations of current technology are described in this chapter, including the presence of software bugs that cause computers to malfunction and the inability of computers to "think" for themselves without the intervention of a human programmer. Many computer scientists today see the natural world as holding the solution to many of these fundamental limitations. This chapter describes research into artificial neural networks, which use computer software modeled on the workings of the human brain, and *evolutionary computation,* which allows computers to solve problems by simulating the process of evolution by natural selection. These and other areas of research that are based on models found in the natural world are examined in this chapter. One of the most interesting of these is *swarm intelligence,* which refers to the collectively intelligent behavior of a group of nonintelligent individuals (such as an ant colony). The concept of swarm intelligence has been incorporated into some software, including CGI software for feature films such as *Batman Returns* and *The Lord of the Rings*. Chapter 8 concludes with a look at how the design of computing systems based on biology is helping researchers learn more about biological processes in the natural world.

As the topics covered in *Computers in Science and Mathematics* illustrate, the technology of computer science as we know it would not exist without the contributions made by countless scientists and mathematicians. Conversely, modern science and mathematics would grind to a halt if computers were unavailable to perform the countless complex computations needed by scientists and mathematicians. Now that computer technology has reached a certain degree of maturity, scientists and mathematicians are no longer pushing the technology forward in a single direction. Instead, humans and computers are influencing each other and enabling each other to progress in a mutually reinforcing feedback loop. *Computers in Science and Mathematics* explores some of the ways in which science, mathematics, and computers have coevolved over time and gives hints as to how they might continue to develop in tandem in the future.

1

BEFORE COMPUTERS: MECHANIZING ARITHMETIC, COUNTING, AND SORTING

It is hard to imagine a time before technology existed for performing calculations. Even using pencil and paper to perform addition by hand involves using technology, primitive as it may be; adding the *digits* in each column and writing the result underneath uses the paper as temporary memory in the process of generating the final sum. Even written number systems, such as the base 10 system of numerals (consisting of the digits 0, 1, 2, 3, 4, 5, 6, 7, 8, and 9), are themselves forms of technology. They are not often thought about as technology simply because they have existed for such a long period of time and have become so ingrained in our relationship to numbers. Today we take for granted not only such seemingly simple tools but also the fast and powerful calculators that are available to use everywhere, from our desktop and laptop computers to our cell phones to our wristwatches.

Nevertheless, there was a time when humans had no physical tools or systematic techniques for counting, performing arithmetic, and carrying out other kinds of mathematical operations. This chapter explores the early history of calculation technology, starting from the time when humans relied solely on their own bodies and the natural phenomena around them to make mathematical sense of the world.

MATHEMATICS BEFORE WRITTEN MATHEMATICAL NOTATION

Counting is one of the historically earliest skills that sets humans apart as a species. The first counting tools were probably human fingers, as evidenced by the fact that the word

1

digit, derived from Latin, can be used to refer either to a number or a finger or toe. When the need arose to count larger numbers of items than was possible using fingers, readily available objects such as rocks, stones, and twigs were put to use. It is not a coincidence that the mathematical terms *calculate* and *calculus* derive from the Latin word for "pebble," *calculus.*

Archaeological artifacts show that humans used early counting tools as far back as 35,000 B.C.E. The oldest of these tools is the Lebombo bone, a primitive tally stick found in Swaziland that was made from the fibula of a baboon and has 29 notches carved into it, possibly representing days in the lunar cycle. The Lebombo bone resembles lunar calendar sticks still used by Bushmen in Namibia. Another artifact, the Ishango bone, has been dated to approximately 20,000 B.C.E. Found in Zaire, this tally stick contains a pattern of notches that suggests it was used as either a calendar counter or primitive *calculator.*

Scientists believe that lunar calendars such as these tally sticks are among the earliest practical uses of counting by humans. Another calendar has been found among prehistoric cave paintings in Lascaux, France. Dating to roughly the same period as the Ishango bone, the painting consists of a series of circles that clearly represent the phases of the Moon.

The meaning of the Ishango bone in terms of the history of mathematics is currently open to interpretation. The existence of other calendar counting devices indicates that it may, in fact, be a calendar, but there are also theories that it was used for simple mathematical functions such as multiplication and division. Unless more evidence in the form of other tools is found, the exact purpose of the Ishango bone will remain something of a mystery.

WRITTEN NUMBER SYSTEMS

When groups of people banded together to form settlements and began to barter and trade, counting with fingers, rocks, and sticks was no longer an adequate way to keep track of numerical quantities. As a result, new tools were devised for tracking and communicating numerical values. Ancient civilizations began to use symbols to represent numbers.

The Babylonians developed one of the earliest number systems around 3000 B.C.E. The Babylonians used a form of writing known as *cuneiform* that consisted of wedge-shaped symbols made with a stick in a wet clay tablet. Many of these tablets have survived, allowing researchers to study the Babylonian system. The

Babylonians used an advanced base 60 number system known as sexigesimal. This is different from our current decimal system, which uses base 10.

Ancient Egyptians practiced several sciences, including chemistry, medicine, and mathematics. The Egyptians used a *decimal number* system and had individual symbols for numbers, called pictographs, that were painted or carved into stone. For example, a single stroke represented the number 1, an arch represented the number 10, and a coiled rope represented the number 100. Ancient Egyptians understood the concept of fractions and had special symbols to represent them. Egyptians are believed to have used advanced mathematics for their achievements in engineering and astronomy, but few records of their methods have survived.

The term *Roman numeral* refers to the number system used by the ancient Romans. The exact origin of this system is unknown. With Roman numerals, letters are used to symbolize base numbers. Letters are combined using addition and subtraction to form any number. For example, "I" represents 1 and "V" represents 5. The number 4 is represented by "IV" (because 5 minus 1 is equal to 4), and 6 is represented by "VI" (because 5 plus 1 is equal to 6). The Roman numeral system has not been used for mathematics for more than 1,000 years because of the difficulty of performing calculations using such numbers, but it still has some limited use today for the display of numbers on clock faces, in copyright dates, and to differentiate items in a series (such as a Super Bowl football game). The main difference between the system of Roman numerals and our current number system is that in Roman numerals, there is no concept of "place value," whereby the value of a digit is determined by its position in a number.

ROMAN NUMERALS AND THEIR DECIMAL EQUIVALENTS	
Roman Numeral	Decimal Equivalent
I	1
V	5
X	10
L	50
C	100
D	500
M	1,000

The concept of place value in numbers was introduced by the Arabic numeral system, in which, for example, "2" has different values in the numbers 20, 200, and 2,000. The Arabic system also introduced symbols that eventually evolved into the modern digits 0, 1, 2, 3, 4, 5, 6, 7, 8, and 9. The Arabic system actually originated in India and was adopted by Arabs around 1000 C.E. It is referred to as "Arabic" because it was introduced to Europeans in the 10th century by Arab scholars from North Africa. The Arabic number system was also the first to introduce the concept of zero.

The Arabic number system is decimal, meaning it uses base 10, and each position in a number represents a power of ten. Numbers are arranged with the lowest value on the right and higher-value positions to the left. This is known as positional notation, and it allows addition, subtraction, and multiplication to be performed far more easily than with earlier number systems.

EARLY MECHANICAL CALCULATORS

A calculator is a device that performs mathematical calculations. Modern calculators are electronic, but mechanical calculators have existed for hundreds of years. The earliest artifact from antiquity that can be described as a calculator is the Antikythera mechanism, a device that is believed to have been used by the ancient Greeks around 150–100 B.C.E. to calculate the motion of stars and planets. The device was discovered in a shipwreck off the isle of Antikythera in 1901 and has been called the most complex scientific object from antiquity. It consists of a bronze plate mounted above 30 miniature geared wheels.

Another early mechanical calculator is Napier's bones, a device that is a form of abacus invented in 1617 by John Napier (1550–1617), a Scottish mathematician, physicist, and astronomer. The device uses a set of numbered rods that have multiplication tables embedded in them to reduce multiplication and division to addition and subtraction. The rods can also be used to calculate square roots.

The Speeding Clock was another early mechanical calculator, devised in 1623 by Wilhelm Schickard (1592–1635), a German scientist. The mechanism could add and subtract six-digit numbers and was used to calculate astronomical tables. According to correspondence from Schickard, the calculator was destroyed in a fire before it was completed. The plans for the Speeding Clock were lost until the 19th century. From these plans, a working replica was constructed in the 1960s.

The Abacus

Centuries before the invention of written number systems, devices were developed to help count large numbers. An abacus is one of these early devices. It was used both for counting and for performing simple operations such as addition and subtraction. A modern abacus consists of a wooden frame with beads on wires that can be moved. Counting is done by changing the position of individual beads.

(continues)

Abacus

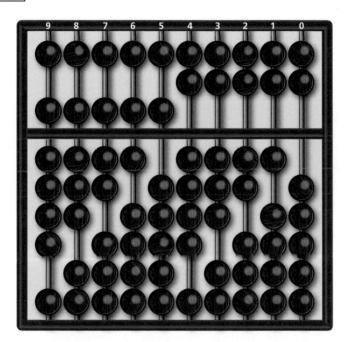

© Infobase Learning

The abacus, one of the oldest devices for counting and performing calculations, has taken many forms in various countries and is still used today. The abacus depicted here shows the digits 9, 8, 7, 6, 5, 4, 3, 2, 1, and 0 from left to right.

(continued)

Originally, an abacus took the form of a counting board, on which small stones were moved in grooves drawn in sand or carved into a wooden board or stone tablet. Evidence of stone and metal counting boards has been found in ancient civilizations, including Babylon, Egypt, Greece, and Rome. In the Middle Ages in Europe, wooden counting boards were used until they were replaced by written numbers and arithmetic, at which point their use declined.

The most familiar form of abacus today originated in China; the earliest reference to it is in Chinese records from 1200 C.E. Known as *suanpan* in China, the modern abacus can be used for operations besides addition and subtraction, including multiplication, division, square roots, and cube roots. In Japan, the abacus was imported from China around 1600 C.E. and is called *soroban*. The *soroban* is taught in Japanese elementary schools as part of the study of mathematics. The effectiveness of the simple abacus device has led to its continuing popularity in Asia as a tool to aid in calculations.

Students using an abacus in Shanghai in 1940   *(AP Images)*

In 1645, Blaise Pascal (1623–62) invented the Pascaline, also known as the *arithmatique.* A French mathematician and philosopher who made major contributions in the fields of physics, mathematics, and economics, Pascal invented the Pascaline when he was 19, possibly to help his father perform calculations more quickly for his job as a tax commissioner. The calculator consisted of a series of dials that were rotated to perform mathematical operations. About a dozen of Pascal's calculators were produced before the high cost of manufacturing and repairing the devices made them unfeasible. The basic design of the Pascaline, however, lives on in modern odometers, which measure distances traveled with rotating dials.

MECHANICAL CALCULATORS IN THE NINETEENTH CENTURY

Mechanical calculators constructed before the 18th century, such as Blaise Pascal's Pascaline, were interesting inventions but did not come into widespread use. Beginning with the Industrial Revolution and increased mechanization, the demand arose for machines that could repeatedly perform accurate calculations. In 1820, Charles-Xavier-Thomas de Colmar (1785–1870), a French inventor and entrepreneur, invented the first mass-produced mechanical calculator. The Arithmometer was a desktop-sized machine that could perform addition, subtraction, multiplication, and division on numbers of up to five digits. Through constant redesign and improvement over a period of decades, Thomas developed the Arithmometer into a commercial success. It was widely used in business from the 1860s until the early 20th century.

In 1887, the American machinist Dorr Felt (1862–1930) invented a mechanical calculator called the Comptometer—the first "key-driven" adding machine to be manufactured and marketed. The Comptometer's key-driven design meant that numbers could be input for calculations simply by pressing a key. For each place value in a number, the Comptometer had a key for each digit from 1–9. Entering a number required the correct key to be pressed for each place. For example, to input "123," an operator would simultaneously depress the 1, 2, and 3 keys in the correct columns.

The main purpose of the Comptometer was to add long lists of numbers, making key-driven entry especially important. The Comptometer quickly became a popular machine for accounting purposes. Because all the keys for

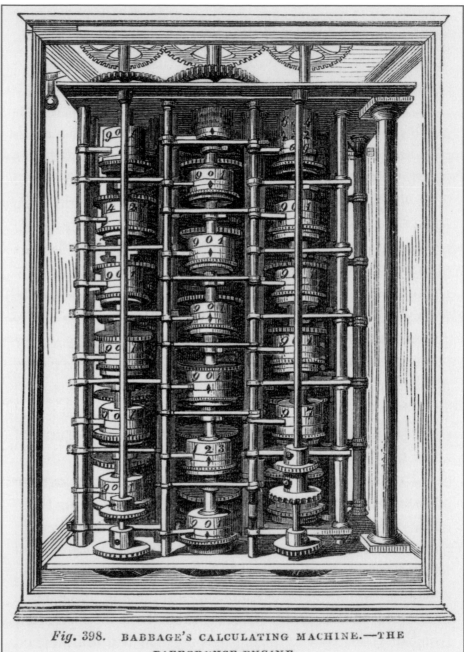

Fig. 398. BABBAGE'S CALCULATING MACHINE.—THE DIFFERENCE-ENGINE.

The Difference Engine, designed by Charles Babbage in 1821, is often considered to be the first automatic calculating machine. *(Mary Evans Picture Library/Alamy)*

a number could be pressed at one time, input by a trained operator using both hands could be done more quickly than with today's *electronic calculators*. Various models of the Comptometer were used by businesses up until the 1970s, when the use of computers for accounting led to their replacement.

In 1821, Charles Babbage (1791–1871), an English mathematician and mechanical engineer, designed the Difference Engine, a calculating machine that used the mathematical principle of finite differences and repeated addition operations to calculate lists of polynomial functions. The Difference Engine has been called the first automatic calculating engine. Babbage's design included a printing mechanism that would print a table of calculated values; between the engine and the printer, the design included 25,000 parts. Work was begun on the Difference Engine but halted in 1832 before the machine was completed. If a working Difference Engine had been produced from the design, it would have been eight feet (2.4 m) tall and weighed about 15 tons (13.6 tonnes).

The section of the Difference Engine that was completed consisted of about 2,000 parts. This section of the engine was operational and continues to be so today. Babbage went on to design another machine called the *Analytical Engine* that would earn him recognition as the father of the modern computer.

THE ANALYTICAL ENGINE

The design of the Analytical Engine is recognized as a milestone in the history of computers. The Analytical Engine moved beyond mechanized arithmetic and calculation to what can truly be called *general-purpose, programmable computing*. Charles Babbage initially conceived of the Analytical Engine in 1837; he would continue to work on the design of the machine until his death in 1871.

The design of the Analytical Engine was a century ahead of its time. Input of instructions and data was to be done using punched cards, a method borrowed from mechanical looms of Babbage's era that used *punched cards* to control the creation of a pattern in woven fabric. *Memory* was included in the Analytical Engine for storing 1,000 50-digit numbers, which was more than any computer designed before 1960 could store. The Analytical Engine included a mill analogous to the *arithmetic logic unit* of a modern computer that would perform the four primary arithmetic operations—addition, subtraction, multiplication, and division—as well as calculate square roots and perform comparisons.

001101010010101001110101101010101011001010100001

Charles Babbage: Inventor of the Nineteenth-Century Computer Known as the Analytical Engine

Charles Babbage was born in Walworth, Surrey, on December 26, 1791, to Benjamin Babbage, a banker, and Elizabeth Teape. Babbage taught himself mathematics, and by the time he entered Cambridge University's Trinity College in 1811, he was more advanced than his teachers in the subject. Babbage graduated from Peterhouse in 1814 and earned a master's degree in 1817.

Charles Babbage designed the Analytical Engine, a programmable automatic calculating machine, in the mid-19th century. Although many consider the Analytical Engine the precursor of modern computers, it was not possible to construct a working Analytical Engine using the manufacturing technology available during Babbage's lifetime. As a result, the Analytical Engine was nearly lost to history until computing pioneers in the mid-20th century rediscovered it. *(Library of Congress)*

Babbage became a mathematician and was elected a Fellow of the Royal Society in 1816. He was an integral participant in the formation of the Royal Astronomical Society in 1820 and taught mathematics at Cambridge, occupying the Lucasian Chair from 1828 to 1839 (this chair is currently occupied by the renowned theoretical physicist Stephen Hawking and earlier by Sir Isaac Newton). The Analytical Society that he cofounded during his years as a student aimed to reform the way mathematics was taught at Cambridge. Babbage helped establish the Association for the Advancement of Science and the Royal Statistical Society and also attempted to convince the government and the public to provide more funding to scientific endeavors, highlighting the neglect of science and the need for more visibility for scientists. Over his lifetime, Babbage published six full-length works and almost

001101010010101001110101101010101011001010100001

90 scientific papers on a variety of scientific topics. He was a man of many interests, ranging from mathematics and science to political economics and philosophy as well as an inventor who pioneered lighthouse signaling and proposed "black boxes" to be used on trains.

However, Babbage's life passion was calculating machinery, which is what created his reputation as a computer pioneer. In 1821, he created his first invention, the Difference Engine, a machine capable of compiling mathematical tables based on the method of finite differences. In the 19th century, calculations were not automated, and mathematical tables, which were relied upon to facilitate calculations, were compiled by hand. However, these tables were full of errors that resulted from the human element of the calculations as well as errors in transcriptions and printing. For example, a random selection of 40 volumes of numerical tables taken in 1834 contained at least 3,700 known errors. Babbage's engine reduced the number of errors because it was capable of both doing the calculations and printing the results, which removed the possibility of human and printing errors. However, by 1834, while the Difference Engine was still unfinished, Babbage had an idea for a machine that would be able to perform any calculation, not just a single task. This machine became known as the Analytical Engine, which is widely regarded as the forefather of the modern computer.

The Analytical Engine included almost all of the essential logical elements of the modern computer. It was programmable, used punch cards, and was able to store numbers and intermediate results as well as to perform any algebraic calculation. The Analytical Engine was capable of "looping," or repeating the same sequence of operations, and "conditional branching," or automatically taking alternative courses of action based on the results of calculations. Had the Analytical Engine been built in Babbage's time, it would have needed a steam engine to operate it.

Unfortunately, very little remains of Babbage's prototype of the Difference Engine, as the machine was too advanced for the technological capabilities of its time. The designs for the Difference Engine called for some 25,000 parts that would have weighed about 16.5 tons (15 tonnes). The machine itself would have been eight feet (2.4 m) tall, seven feet (2.1 m) long, and three feet (0.9 m) wide. Babbage hired the British engineer Joseph Clement (1779–1844) to assist in the

(continues)

(continued)

construction of the Difference Engine. Clement completed a portion of the Difference Engine in 1832; this construction remains the oldest scientific calculator and is regarded to be one of the finest examples of 19th-century engineering. However, the British government halted funding for the project due to the technological impediments to its creation, and Babbage spent a considerable amount of his own money on unsuccessful further attempts at constructing the engine. Between 1847 and 1849, using designs for his Analytical Engine, Babbage designed an improved Difference Engine, which required only a third of the number of parts of the original Difference Engine to achieve the same computing power. However, he never tried to build it. Babbage was deeply disappointed by the government's refusal to support his work. He died in 1871 at his home in London without seeing his invention's success. Babbage's son Henry Prevost Babbage continued his father's work after Babbage's death, but the engine was never successfully completed and was able to run only very few error-filled programs.

The Science Museum of London, which holds the most comprehensive set of Babbage's original manuscripts and design drawings, completed the construction of the second Difference Engine in 1991, 200 years after Babbage's birth, using what was left of the original designs in order to see whether it was the limitation of the engineering science of Babbage's day that contributed to the failure of his project. The calculating section of the engine consists of 4,000 parts and weighs ca. 2.9 tons (2.6 tonnes), stands seven feet (2.1 m) tall, 11 feet (3.4 m) long, and 18 inches (45.7 cm) wide, and is built of materials that would have been available to Babbage. Although modern techniques were used for manufacturing the parts, their precision was purposefully limited to what would have been possible in Babbage's time. The printer for the engine was completed in 2000 and weighs ca. 2.8 tons (2.5 tonnes).

In addition to mathematical functions, the Analytical Engine was designed to perform many other operations used by modern computers, including branching, looping, and *parallel processing*. Babbage also conceived of a programming language for the Analytical Engine that was similar to current low-level languages known as assembly languages.

Due to a variety of problems, both financial and legal, a working version of the Analytical Engine was not built in Babbage's lifetime. Many scientists believe that the machine was too complex to be built using the manufacturing methods of Babbage's era. Despite the lack of a physical model from Babbage's time, the design for the Analytical Engine has been studied in detail and is recognized as a landmark among intellectual achievements of the 19th century.

CONCLUSIONS

At first glance, it might seem that there is little connection between the way in which people perform mathematical calculations, whether in their heads or using pencil and paper, and the way in which mechanical calculating machines, such as mechanical cash registers and Babbage's Analytical Engine, perform arithmetic and other computations on numbers. Open a mechanical calculator and one will not see a living, pulsing brain but instead a collection of shafts, levers, and gears that can achieve the same end result as a human calculator—such as concluding that $3 \times 2 = 6$—using what appears to be a completely different mechanism, just as an automobile engine can perform the same work as a horse, but by using belts and pistons rather than flesh and bone.

These obvious distinctions between how humans and machines perform calculations obscure some important similarities. Although no mechanical calculator contains anything resembling a human brain, the unaided and untrained human brain can perform only very limited calculations. People who have never been taught how to perform arithmetic can typically add only very small numbers to each other, such as $2 + 3$, and only then by using their fingers or forming a mental image in which they combine stones or other physical objects together to find the answer. Adding larger numbers, particularly those containing more than two or three digits, requires previous memorization of the answers to simpler addition problems and previous training in how to follow rules for adding large numbers to each other.

Consider, for example, the process of adding $347 + 271$. Most people are taught in grade school to find the answer using a particular algorithm in which the two numbers are written down on paper, one on top of the other, with the columns of both numbers aligned with each other. The numbers in each column are then added to each other, beginning with the rightmost column, and the

Grade School Addition Algorithm

The sequence of steps taught to students in grade school for adding numbers by adding individual columns of digits is an example of an "algorithm."

© Infobase Learning

resulting sums are written directly beneath the columns that produced them. Even the simple step of adding two single-digit numbers to each other (such as 7 and 1) typically requires previous memorization of "addition tables," so that the answer (8, in this case) can be recalled immediately from memory rather than calculated from scratch. Each succeeding column of numbers is processed in the same way. If any individual sum of two numbers is more than 9, a special "carry" rule is followed, in which the "carry digit" (such as "1" in the case of the number 10) is written above the column immediately to the left of the current column, such that the carry digit is added to the sum of the column beneath it. After the numbers in the leftmost column have been summed, the multidigit number (618 in this example) that has been written beneath the original two numbers (347 and 271 in this example) represents their sum.

Few people could perform such addition using their brains alone. Instead, it is the combination of memorized addition tables, a memorized set of rules (algorithm) for performing addition, and the use of pencil and paper as a temporary scratchpad and final recording medium for the sum that makes it impossible for all but the most gifted of human calculators to add anything other than single-digit numbers to each other. Anyone who doubts the significance of pencil and paper in this process can test their mettle by attempting to add two very long numbers, such as 89,253,423,461 and 17,726,381,819, to each other with their eyes closed.

A person who performs addition using this grade school addition algorithm does so in much the same way that a computer performs addition. Both humans and computers first memorize the answers to very simple, single-digit addition problems. Both humans and computers then memorize a rigid set of rules for adding large numbers to each other and apply those rules to any particular pair of numbers provided to them, using a temporary scratchpad, and store the final result in an external recording medium that can then be read by a person to obtain the desired answer. There are significant differences in the details of how humans and computers perform these steps. For example, humans perform addition using decimal (base 10) numbers with digits ranging from 0 to 9, while computers typically perform addition using binary (base 2) numbers with bits ranging from 0 to 1. Humans use a pencil and paper to add and record numbers, while computers use electronic *processors* and memory to perform the same functions. Such differences in details of implementation should not, however, obscure the fundamental similarities between human-performed and computer-performed calculations.

These similarities are not coincidental: They result from many of the same driving forces and have many of the same effects. Mathematicians originally created algorithms for carrying out arithmetic to make it possible for people to perform more complex calculations more easily and quickly and with less understanding of mathematics than was previously required. The grade school addition algorithm achieves these goals spectacularly. Just consider that a child can use the algorithm to add numbers such as 89,253,423,461 and 17,726,381,819 to produce the sum of 106,979,805,280 in less than a minute without understanding why the grade school algorithm produces the right answer and without being able to comprehend the value of 106,979,805,280. It is even possible to teach someone to use the grade school algorithm to add numbers accurately without that person knowing that what they are doing is adding numbers. Instead, someone can follow the rules of the algorithm to happily write the correct sequence of digits underneath two large numbers without ever knowing that the resulting digit sequence represents the sum of the two starting numbers.

Algorithms such as the grade school addition algorithm therefore systematize processes such as addition so that such processes can be carried out by rote, that is, merely by rigidly following rules without understanding why those rules work or even what their purpose is. When a human carries out such an algorithm, we often say that he or she does so "mechanically" or "like a machine." The existence of such algorithms makes it possible to create machines that can carry out such algorithms and thereby perform computations. Algorithms of this kind, in other words, enable humans to perform calculations in a machine-like manner and also enable machines to perform calculations without needing to have the human qualities of creativity, discretion, and understanding. More generally, the act of systematizing a process such as addition by reducing it to a rigid set of rules often makes it possible for people to perform that process using only a certain mechanical kind of skill and simultaneously opens the door to automating the same process using machines. In the end, the ways in which humans and machines perform calculations is not always that different after all.

2

EARLY COMPUTERS: AUTOMATING COMPUTATION

Charles Babbage's failed effort to construct the Analytical Engine remained the primary attempt to design and build a fully automated programmable computer for several decades. In fact, Babbage's work largely faded from memory and was nearly lost to history until computing pioneers rediscovered it in the 1930s. Although automatic, electronic, programmable computers of the kind originally envisioned by Babbage were eventually created, they were the result of a long and winding path that did not lead straight from Babbage's door. Instead, innovators after Babbage initially took quite a different approach by developing special purpose machines designed to tackle particular real-world calculation problems. Gradually, over many years, the features of such machines were modified, improved, expanded, and combined with one another, resulting not merely in a working version of Babbage's Analytical Engine but in fully electronic computers that far exceeded in speed and versatility anything that Babbage had designed. This chapter reviews the first steps on the path from the Analytical Engine to modern computers.

THE HOLLERITH TABULATOR

In 1890, an American inventor, Herman Hollerith (1860–1929), designed an electrical tabulating machine for use in the 1890 United States Census. The demand arose after tabulating the 1880 census took seven years. In addition to being time consuming, the process of hand tabulation was expensive and prone to error. Due to a surge in the U.S. population, the 1890 census was expected to take 13 years to process, meaning the information from the 1890 census would be obsolete before it could be completely processed. Since the U.S. Constitution requires a census to be conducted once every decade to determine congressional representation and the division of taxes, it became clear that a faster approach to processing census data was needed.

Hollerith chose punched cards as the medium for recording census data. Punched cards had been used in the past for controlling machine operation; examples include the Jacquard loom and the piano roll used by automatic player pianos. *Hollerith's tabulating machine* was the first to use them for data entry (although Charles Babbage previously had proposed such use). The design of his punched card consisted of small markers laid out in 12 rows with 24 columns per row. A small oval hole could be punched in a marker position. The tabulating machine used electrical relays and circuits to determine the location of punched holes on a card and then to increment an appropriate mechanical counter. For the 1890 census, Hollerith's punched cards contained information about an individual's age, gender, home state, and other personal characteristics.

The Census Office leased tabulating machines from Hollerith, and census data processing was completed ahead of schedule and under budget. Hollerith's invention had revolutionized census tabulation. Following the 1890 census, the Census Office developed its own in-house version of the tabulating machine. Hollerith continued to lease his machines to census bureaus around the world as well as to insurance companies.

In 1896, Hollerith formed the Tabulating Machine Company. Over a period of two decades, a series of mergers and management changes led to Hollerith's company becoming the International Business Machine Corporation (IBM). This corporation was to become the dominant force in computer design, manufacturing, sales, and consulting for most of the 20th century.

To make his tabulating machine more suited to general purposes, Hollerith introduced a control panel to the 1906 model of his Type I Tabulator. This control panel made it possible for the machine to perform different types of operations without being rebuilt. Hollerith's control panel is viewed as one of the early precursors to programmable machine control. Hollerith's tabulator and his use of punched cards laid the foundation for the commercialization of large-scale information processing.

THE HARVARD MARK I

In 1944, IBM delivered the first large-scale automatic digital computer to Harvard University. The electromechanical machine was initially known as the

The Bombe: The Decryption Machine That Ended World War II

In the years during World War II, most German military communications were transmitted in encoded form using an electromechanical cipher machine called the Enigma machine. The German military believed that the encrypted messages that were produced by the Enigma were impossible to break, in part because the configuration of the Enigma's multiple rotors needed to be matched exactly to decipher Enigma-encrypted messages. The number of possible configurations was very large, and the German military frequently changed the configuration that it used to transmit encrypted messages.

(continues)

Decryption Using a Bombe

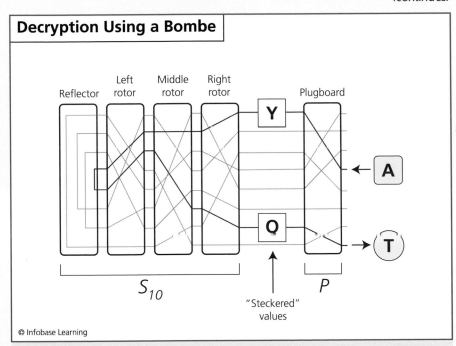

© Infobase Learning

During World War II, the British mathematicians Alan Turing and Gordon Welchman designed the Bombe, which was capable of decrypting messages transmitted by the German Enigma encryption machine. The Bombe is credited with shortening the length of World War II by months, if not years.

001101010010100111010110101010101011001010000 1

(continued)

As the German military became more aggressive in its attacks, Britain began hiring mathematicians for its Government Code & Cipher School (GC&CS). Two mathematicians from Cambridge, Alan Turing and Gordon Welchman, joined the GC&CS team in 1939. By 1940, the pair had designed a machine known as the British Bombe that could break the code of any Enigma message. A large measure of the Bombe's success was due to earlier work by the Polish cryptanalyst Marian Rejewski and to the capture of Enigma codebooks from German military forces. The first model of the Bombe machine, built by an engineer from the British Tabulating Machine Company named Harold Keen, took several months to complete. Eventually, the construction time was reduced to a week, and in total 210 Bombes were built for use during the war.

Each Bombe weighed one ton, was six feet (1.8 m) tall and seven feet (2.1 m) long, and consisted of 36 sets of three rotors. The principle used by the Bombe involved working exhaustively through rotor settings in the opposite direction from the Enigma. An electrical current was applied to determine if the setting of the rotors was a match to the Enigma settings for a given message. When a match was found, the machine was stopped and the rotor settings were noted and used to decipher the message.

Throughout the war, the British Bombe machines and similar machines in the United States were the principal method used to break the code of Enigma-encrypted messages. The information gleaned from these messages was a major contributing factor to the Allied victory.

001101010010100111010110101010101011001010000 1

Automatic Sequence Controlled Calculator (ASCC) but came to be known as the *Harvard Mark I computer*. It was designed by Howard H. Aiken and a team of scientists that included Grace Hopper, who was a pioneer in computer programming. The Mark I represents a milestone in computing since it was the first universal calculator that could perform calculations fully automatically, without human intervention.

The Harvard Mark I was controlled by punched paper tape. Data for calculation could be input by paper tape, punched cards, or control switches. This early computer supported basic arithmetic functions (addition, subtraction, multiplication, and division) as well as storing and referencing the answers from previous calculations. Preprogrammed subroutines supported logarithms and trigonometric functions. Numbers with up to 23 decimal places could be used for calculations. One of the important advances made with the Mark I was its ability to retain mathematical rules in memory, eliminating the need for reprogramming for each new set of problems.

The Mark I used electromagnetic relays for computing and storing data, and output was displayed on an electric typewriter. The computer weighed five tons (4.5 tonnes), was 51 feet (15.5 m) long and eight feet (2.4 m) tall, and consisted of more than 750,000 separate parts. It essentially consisted of 78 adding machines and calculators linked together with wire and relays. With all of its pieces made of metal, the Mark I was noisy and somewhat slow; a simple arithmetic operation could take up to five seconds.

The Mark I was initially used by the U.S. Navy for ballistic calculations. After World War II ended, it continued to operate until 1959 and was used for complex calculations in a variety of disciplines.

THE ENIAC: THE FIRST MODERN COMPUTER

The ENIAC (Electronic Numerical Integrator and Computer) was announced in 1946 as the first large-scale general-purpose electronic computer. The ENIAC was called general purpose because it could be programmed to compute a wide range of different problems. It was able to complete 5,000 addition operations in one second, faster than the electromechanical calculators of its time by a factor of a thousand.

The design and construction of the ENIAC was funded by the U.S. Army during World War II. It was designed by John Mauchly (1907–80) and J. Presper Eckert (1919–95) of the University of Pennsylvania. The total cost for design and construction was roughly $500,000 (equivalent to about $6 million in 2010 dollars). The ENIAC was installed at the Aberdeen Proving Ground in Maryland in 1947 and operated continuously until it was immobilized by lightning in 1955. While it was operational, it was used for computations related to the hydrogen bomb as well as weather prediction, random-number studies, wind tunnel design, and other scientific and military projects.

The ENIAC was notable for its size. It contained almost 18,000 vacuum tubes, weighed 30 tons (27.2 tonnes), and was almost 80 feet (24.4 m) long. Data input

J. Presper Eckert (foreground left) and John W. Mauchly (leaning against pole) standing amidst components of their invention, the ENIAC (Electronic Numerical Integrator and Computer) that could perform 5,000 addition operations in one second at the time of its creation in 1946. *(AP Images)*

was performed via punched cards and a card reader; data output was also done with punched cards. The ENIAC used the base 10 decimal system rather than the binary system that came to be used by the majority of subsequent computers.

The programmability of the ENIAC allowed a series of operations to be performed in a sequence. A primitive form of conditional execution was provided by loops and branches. This was an improvement over the earlier Mark I computer, which had no support for conditionals. However, one of the great shortcomings of the ENIAC was its inability to store programs. Each time a program was to be executed, it had to be reentered into the ENIAC using switches on the front panel. The process of developing and entering program instructions into the computer was painstaking and time consuming. Programming at that time was viewed as a clerical task and was completed by a team of six women.

The design of the ENIAC was never replicated or carried forward to another computer. Its most important contribution to the history of computers was in the proof that a large-scale, fast, and powerful computer could be built and that vacuum tube technology could support digital computing. Mauchly and Eckert subsequently designed another type of computer, named the EDVAC, that would compensate for many of the shortcomings of the ENIAC.

THE EDVAC: THE VON NEUMANN ARCHITECTURE

The EDVAC (Electronic Discrete Variable Automatic Computer) followed the ENIAC as one of the earliest electronic computers. Unlike the ENIAC, which had a decimal architecture, the EDVAC was a binary machine. Another major difference between the ENIAC and EDVAC was that the EDVAC could store programs so that they would not have to be reentered to be used more than once.

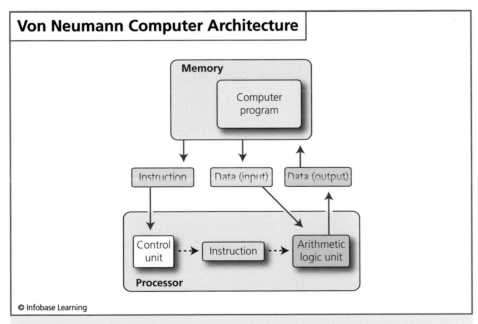

Von Neumann Computer Architecture

© Infobase Learning

The von Neumann architecture, named after its designer, John von Neumann, incorporates a memory that stores a computer program and a processor that reads instructions from the memory and then executes the instructions. Von Neumann first proposed this architecture in 1945, and it still serves as the foundation for most computers today.

The developers of the ENIAC, John Mauchly and J. Presper Eckert, began work on the EDVAC before the ENIAC was completed. In 1945, the mathematician John von Neumann (1903–57) created a formal description of a stored-program digital computer as part of the development of EDVAC. This description included a processing unit and a separate storage unit to hold both data and program instructions. This form of computer architecture became known as the *von Neumann architecture* and was used in the design of the EDVAC. Since then, it has been used as the architecture for almost all computers.

The EDVAC was more powerful and faster than the ENIAC. It was also smaller, with 6,000 vacuum tubes and a weight of about nine tons (8.2 tonnes) compared to about 18,000 tubes and 30 tons (27.2 tonnes) for the ENIAC. It was completed in 1949 and continued to operate at the Ballistics Research Laboratory at the Aberdeen Proving Ground in Maryland until 1961.

FROM SPECIAL-PURPOSE TO GENERAL-PURPOSE COMPUTERS

Most machines are designed to do just one thing and to do it well. A microwave oven cooks food. A car transports its driver from home to work. A microwave oven will never take a person to work, and a car will never cook food. As a result, such devices are called special-purpose or single-function machines because each one serves only one purpose and performs only one function.

Many special-purpose devices, such as knives, are designed to perform functions so narrow that they can only be used to perform their basic function, such as cutting, in very limited circumstances. For example, a steak knife excels at cutting steak but not at chopping onions, while a paring knife can be used to strip the skin off an apple but not to slice bread. As a result, much of what inventors have done throughout history is to tweak the designs of existing machines to make them effective for performing the wide variety of functions needed by people at home and at work. The engineering professor Henry Petroski has written several books chronicling the hundreds of varieties of everyday objects, such as spoons and paperclips, that have been designed over the centuries to carry out incredibly narrow but important functions.

Some devices can do many different things. A Swiss army knife, for example, can whittle wood, uncork a wine bottle, and fasten a screw. Such devices are known as multifunction devices. A more contemporary example of a multi-function machine is a combination printer-scanner-fax-copier, now commonly found connected to many people's computers.

Although one might think that multifunction machines are always more desirable than special-purpose machines—that more necessarily is better—that is not always the case. It is true that a combination printer-scanner takes up less room on a desk and is less expensive than purchasing a printer and a scanner separately. On the other hand, the quality of the printer in a combination printer-scanner is usually lower than the quality of a comparably priced standalone printer. The same is true of the scanner. Furthermore, the standalone printer probably has a control panel that is better suited to a printer and easier to use than the combination printer-scanner.

Multifunction machines, however, do have some clear benefits, particularly for mathematicians, scientists, and engineers. Early calculating machines, for example, could perform only a very limited set of calculations. A particular calculating machine might be capable of performing only addition, while another calculating machine might be capable of performing only division. If an engineer wanted to calculate the results of an equation that involved performing both addition and division, she would need to use two different calculating machines. This was very tedious and frustrating. Eventually, calculating machines were developed that could perform a combination of addition, subtraction, multiplication, division, and other mathematical operations. This made life much easier for those whose work relied on performing large numbers of complex calculations.

Early versions of such calculating machines, however, could perform only one mathematical operation at a time under the manual control of the user. To use such a machine to calculate the results of an equation, one would need to calculate each part of the equation separately and then combine them together. For example, to calculate the value of x in the equation $x = 9 + (3 \times 2) - 8$, one would need to use the machine to multiply 3×2, then use the machine to add the result to 9, then use the machine to subtract 8 from the result. Eventually, calculating machines were designed to calculate the result of an entire equation automatically.

The problem with those improved machines, however, was that they could only calculate the result of only one particular equation. If one needed to calculate the results of several different equations, one would either need to modify an existing calculating machine or use several different calculating machines, one for calculating each equation.

These examples illustrate a pattern. The earliest calculating machines were designed to perform only a very specific function, such as adding two numbers together. As mathematicians, scientists, and engineers became frustrated with the limitations of such machines, they designed new calculating machines that could perform an even wider range of calculations. This process repeated over and over again, leading first to calculating machines that could perform any mathematical operation, then to calculating machines that could calculate entire equations, and then to calculating machines that could calculate the result of any equation.

A machine that is capable of performing any possible combination of mathematical operations is difficult to classify as a "special-purpose machine" because it can perform so many different functions. In fact, the British mathematician Alan Turing wrote a paper in 1936 in which he described the possibility of a machine

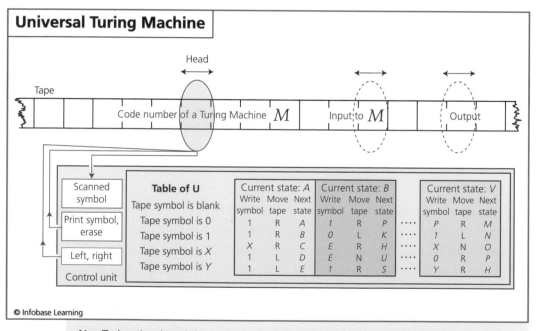

© Infobase Learning

Alan Turing developed the concept of a universal machine, which could mimic the function of any other computing machine. The basic operation of Turing's universal machine serves as the foundation for nearly all modern computers. As a result, the universal machine is called the Universal Turing Machine in honor of Turing's contribution.

that could perform not only any mathematical operation but also any possible manipulation of symbols (such as adding the string of symbols "def" to the string of symbols "abc" to produce "abcdef"). He referred to this machine as a *universal machine* because it was so general that it could mimic the behavior of any other machine for performing calculations or for manipulating symbols more generally. Turing originally envisioned the program for a universal machine being stored on a tape along with the input to the program. The universal machine would read the instructions from the tape, carry out the computations described by the instructions, and write the resulting output to the end of the tape.

Today's computers are real-world examples of Turing's universal machine. A computer can be made to perform a nearly infinite number of functions. One can see this every time a new piece of software is installed onto a computer. Performing such an installation transforms the computer into a modified version of itself that can perform a new function. Install videogame software onto a computer and the computer becomes capable of playing the videogame; the same is true of tax software, Web browsing software, and word processing software.

As these examples illustrate, a computer—a universal machine—is made to perform a particular function by installing the right software onto the computer. A piece of software is sometimes called a "program," and as a result the act of installing software onto a computer is a way of programming the computer, even if the person who installs the software did not write the software. Because today's computers can be programmed to perform essentially any function, computers are sometimes called general-purpose programmable computers to distinguish them from the special-purpose, nonprogrammable machines that our ancestors had to tolerate.

ELECTRONIC PROCESSORS AND MEMORY MAKE MODERN COMPUTERS POSSIBLE

Following development of the ENIAC and EDVAC computers, innovation in the area of computer hardware design continued at a rapid pace throughout the 1940s and 1950s. Electronic computers based on vacuum tube technology became commercially available. In the early 1950s, the Remington Rand Univac I was used by the U.S. Census Bureau and other large organizations. In total, 46 units of the Univac I were sold at a cost of about $1 million each.

(continues on page 31)

Alan Turing: Creator of the Concept of the Modern Computer and Inventor of Early Computers

Alan Turing was born in 1912 in Paddington, London, the second child of Julius Mathison Turing and Ethel Turing. Julius Turing served in the Indian Civil Service, and both Alan and his brother John grew up in a variety of English homes until their father's retirement from India in 1926. Creativity and curiosity were not encouraged by Alan's upbringing, and science became his extracurricular passion, first manifested by primitive chemistry experiments. Turing credited a popular book entitled *Natural Wonders Every Child Should Know* as a major influence on his childhood scientific pursuits. Tur-

Alan Turing was a British mathematician, engineer, and philosopher whose publications and designs in the mid-20th century laid the groundwork for modern computers. *(Science Photo Library/Photo Researchers, Inc.)*

ing's mother was concerned that her son's scientific passion would make him unacceptable to the public school system and thus put them at odds with the expectations of the family's middle class societal obligations. However, Alan was enrolled at Sherborne, a private school, where he met and befriended Christopher Morcom, who provided Turing with much-needed intellectual companionship and scientific encouragement. Morcom's sudden death two years later prompted Turing's inquiries into the workings of the human mind and its relationship to matter and whether the mind can be released from the matter by death. These questions in turn led him to study physics.

Turing next attended Kings College at Cambridge University, where he earned a degree with distinction, followed by a fellowship at Kings College and a Smith's Prize in 1936 for his work on probability theory. All seemed in place for Turing to have a successful career as a mathematician. Instead, Turing turned to exploration of mathematical logic through the works of Bertrand Russell, A. N. Whitehead, and Kurt Gödel. This led Turing to explore the question of whether there was a method by which it could be determined if a mathematical assertion were provable. Turing theorized that a "definite method" could be a mechanical process performed by a machine, that is, an elementary operation on symbols recorded on paper tape. He analogized this process to the workings of a human mind. Turing's "definite method" became known as an algorithm in modern terms. The concept of his theoretical machine working with paper tape, however, known as the Turing Machine, became the foundation of the modern computer.

In particular, Turing introduced the idea of a Universal Turing Machine. If any particular Turing Machine can be made to compute its own specific "definite method," and if each such definite method can be expressed as a set of instructions in standard form, then interpreting the instructions and following them itself becomes a mechanical process. As a result, it is possible to encode the instructions that define any particular Turing Machine and to provide those instructions to a Universal Turing Machine. The Universal Turing Machine, when it executes the instructions, behaves as if it is the particular Turing Machine defined by the instructions. As a result, only the Universal Turning Machine is needed to perform any task so long as the task can be reduced to and expressed through instructions in standard form. This concept of instructions being represented by symbols is very similar to the later computing concept of symbols representing numbers. However, computers in the modern sense did not exist in 1936, and Turing's Universal Machine remained theoretical.

Turing continued his studies at Princeton, where for two years he worked on algebra and number theory and received a Ph.D. for his work on ordinal logics. However, he abandoned all work in this area after 1938. Instead, he focused on other logical problems. While at Princeton and influenced by the possibility of war with Germany, Turing developed a cipher machine that used electromagnetic relays to multiply *binary numbers*. Upon returning to Britain, he worked part time for the British Cryptoanalytic Department and did research on breaking

(continues)

(continued)

the German mechanical Enigma cipher. Upon Britain's declaration of war, Turing continued to work full-time for the Cryptoanalytic Department and was a driving force behind the successful breaking of the Enigma cipher.

In 1944, relying on the developments in electronic technology brought about by the necessities of the war with Germany, Turing was able to bring to life his idea of the Universal Turing Machine. He was motivated to overcome the inefficiency of designing individual machines tailored to a specific task and was therefore eager to implement his idea for one machine capable of any programmable task. Turing was also motivated by the possibility that his universal machine might be able to mimic the human brain; in fact, he spoke of "building a brain" when referring to his creation, the Automatic Computing Engine (ACE).

Turing knew that advances in technology would soon transform his design, but it was his vision for the application and usage of the computer that was revolutionary. His 1947 Abbreviated Code Instructions became the prototype for later programming languages, but Turing was forced out of the engineering of the final project. He returned to Cambridge to do research on neurological and physiological issues, which culminated in a paper revisiting his earlier theory that a complex enough mechanical system can have learning abilities similar to those of a human mind. However, this paper was not published in Turing's lifetime.

In 1948, Turing accepted the post of deputy director of the computing laboratory at Manchester University. During this time, Turing worked on "Computing Machinery and Intelligence," a paper that summarized his views on the philosophy of computing and cognition, which was published by the philosophical journal *Mind* in 1950. In 1951, he was elected to the fellowship of the Royal Society for all his previous contributions. Later that year, Turing produced yet another notable paper entitled "The Chemical Basis of Morphogenesis," which became the foundation of modern nonlinear dynamical theory. He also revisited his youthful interest in quantum physics.

Turing was found dead by his cleaner on June 8, 1954, of cyanide poisoning. Although his mother believed his death was an accident from ingesting cyanide from his fingers following a chemistry experiment, the coroner's conclusion was suicide.

(continued from page 27)

There were many drawbacks associated with vacuum tubes, including their size, fragility, and high power consumption. The transistor was invented in 1948 and soon replaced the vacuum tube in computers due its more compact size, lower cost, decreased power consumption, and increased reliability. In 1956, researchers at the Massachusetts Institute of Technology (MIT) produced the TX-0, a general-purpose programmable computer that used transistors rather than vacuum tubes. IBM produced a line of mainframe computers that used transistors in 1959.

Following the introduction of transistors, a new class of computers known as supercomputers became available. A supercomputer called the CDC 6600 was introduced in 1964. Designed by Seymour Cray, it could perform up to 3 million operations per second, a figure that was triple the speed of its closest competitor. The design of the CDC 6600 consisted of 10 smaller computers, the peripheral processors, feeding the results of intermediate computations to a larger *central processing unit.* True parallel processing in a computer was introduced in the early 1970s by the Department of Defense with its ILLIAC computer, which could perform 300 million operations per second.

Transistors required complicated wiring, which had to be done by hand. In the mid-1960s, transistors began to be replaced by integrated circuits. An integrated circuit includes transistors and wiring in a single component, referred to as a chip. In the mid-1970s, early personal computers based on integrated circuits began to appear. In 1975, *Popular Electronics* magazine featured its Altair personal computer kit, and in 1976, Steve Wozniak and Steve Jobs designed the first Apple personal computer.

Improvements in the technology used for computer memory, from vacuum tubes to transistors to integrated circuits, led both to vast improvements in speed and performance and to miniaturization of computer components. These improvements made possible the compact, powerful computers and smart devices that are commonplace today.

CONCLUSIONS

Today's computers are used for such a wide variety of purposes—browsing the Web, sending and receiving e-mail, writing documents, playing games—that it is easy to forget that computers were originally used solely to "compute"—to perform calculations on numbers. The ability of early computers to perform calculations quickly and accurately caused them to be adopted by government agencies, large corporations, and universities, which used them for everything from compiling accounting reports to predicting the trajectories of missiles to charting the paths of the stars. Most early users of computers were perfectly content to use them solely as number-crunching machines. Even most designers of computers well into the 1960s did not see any reason to attempt to use computers for anything other than performing calculations within large organizations. Only a few far-sighted pioneers at that time envisioned users having individual computers on their own desktops to perform noncalculation tasks, such as creating business documents and databases.

The incredible versatility of today's computers makes it easy to see them as universal machines. It is possible to purchase or even download for free software that can perform nearly any task for today's personal computers. Technological "convergence" is increasingly blurring the dividing line between computers, telephones, personal digital assistants (PDAs), televisions, and other electronic equipment as each becomes capable of performing all of the functions of the other devices combined. Today, someone with a handheld "smartphone" that weighs just a few ounces can run all of the same software and perform all of the same functions that required a separate desktop computer, PDA, and landline-connected telephone just a few years ago, and at a fraction of the cost.

Such power and flexibility can make it easy to overlook how even the earliest computers, which were used only to perform calculations—and to do even that quite slowly by today's standards—had still crossed the line from special-purpose machines to general-purpose (universal) machines. To understand why, consider a machine that straddles the boundary line between special-purpose and general-purpose machines: a power drill with interchangeable bits. On one hand, such a drill is a special-purpose machine, because the only function it can perform is to spin its motor when power is applied to it. On the other hand, one can change the function the drill performs by attaching different drill bits to it. Attach a drilling bit to the drill, and it behaves like a drill. Attach a screwdriver bit to the drill, and it behaves like a screwdriver. Attach a sanding bit to the drill, and it behaves like a sander. Although such a drill is not truly "general purpose" or "universal" because it is limited to performing tasks that can be powered by a rotating motor, it is much more adaptable than a truly single-purpose drill, which has only a single, nondetachable bit connected to it.

In one sense, computer hardware is to computer software as drills are to drill bits. Just as a drill without any bits attached to it will spin furiously but do nothing useful, a computer without any software installed on it will do nothing but consume power. Similarly, just as installing a Phillips-head screwdriver bit in a drill enables the drill to screw Phillips-head screws, so too does installing tax software on a computer enable the computer to prepare tax returns. Each new piece of software that is installed on a computer enables it to perform a new function.

One important difference, however, between a drill and a computer lies not in how drill bits and software *work,* but in how they are *designed.* Drill bits are typically designed by mechanical engineers using their knowledge of the laws of physics and by drawing diagrams and testing prototypes of drill bits until they arrive at a design that works as desired. Software, in contrast, is designed by computer programmers by writing programs that contain instructions that describe the actions the software is intended to perform. Computer programmers, as a result, can make computers perform new functions merely by writing descriptions of those functions in an appropriate programming language.

This ability to control computers by providing them with written instructions conferred significant advantages, even in the days when they were capable only of performing calculations. Consider an astronomer who needed to use various equations to calculate the paths of different stars or even to calculate the path of the same star on different days. Before programmable computers existed, calculating the results of such distinct equations might require physically rewiring a calculating machine for each equation. Doing so was not only tedious and time consuming, it required the astronomer to have some understanding of the calculating machine's wiring and how to change that wiring to calculate different equations accurately. The advent of computers that could be programmed using written instructions meant that the same astronomer could achieve the same effect as rewiring the computer but instead by merely typing in each desired equation to the computer in a mathematical language that the astronomer already understood, without requiring any understanding of electrical circuitry. Although we take for granted today this ability to bend computers to our will using instructions, it represented a great leap forward in the use of machines to perform calculations quickly and easily.

3

CRYPTOGRAPHY: SENDING SECRET MESSAGES

People often want or need to tell each other secrets. Telling a secret to another person orally is easy—just make sure that no one is in earshot, then say the secret out loud. Even if one is in a crowded room, secrecy usually can be maintained simply by whispering rather than speaking at a normal volume.

It becomes more difficult, however, to communicate a message orally to someone else over a long distance. If one opens a window and shouts to a neighbor across the street, it is difficult to ensure that no one else nearby will overhear the message. Similarly, communicating messages in writing rather than orally makes it more difficult to ensure that only the person to whom the message is addressed reads it, both because it is possible that an eavesdropper will intercept the message on its way to the recipient and because the recipient may not destroy the written message after reading it.

For these and other reasons, people for thousands of years have attempted to scramble written messages to make them difficult to read. A scrambled message is useless unless the person to whom it is addressed knows how to unscramble it. The processes of scrambling and descrambling messages to ensure that only the sender and intended recipient of the message can read it are also known as encryption and decryption. The study of encryption and decryption is known as cryptography.

Students often develop their own simple encryption systems for passing notes to friends in class. One method that many people think of on their own involves shifting letters in the alphabet in one direction to encrypt a message and then shifting letters back in the opposite direction to decrypt the message. The simplest version of this technique is to encrypt a message by shifting each letter in the message up by one letter, so that A becomes B, B becomes C, C becomes D, and so on. (Upon reaching the letter Z, one "wraps around" to the beginning again to produce the letter A.) In this case, the message "hello" would become "ifmmp." The original message is known as *plaintext* and the encrypted message is known as *ciphertext.* As can be seen from this example, even an extremely simple encryption scheme can produce ciphertext that is difficult for an eavesdropper to read if he or she does not know how the ciphertext was produced and how to reverse the encryption process to recreate the original plaintext, in this case by shifting each letter in the ciphertext "ifmmp" down by one to produce "hello."

This kind of encryption scheme is not suitable for protecting important information, however, because it is too easy to "crack," meaning that an eavesdropper who obtains access to an encrypted message, such as the ciphertext "ifmmp," can easily use that ciphertext to figure out how to decrypt the ciphertext to produce the original plaintext and then to decrypt any subsequent pieces of ciphertext obtained. Although it might take one a long time to deduce that "ifmmp" is simply "hello" shifted by one letter, computer software can easily look at the ciphertext "ifmmp" and, in a fraction of a second, attempt to decrypt the message by applying all possible letter-shifts to "ifmmp" and then conclude that the amount of the shift is +1. Computer software has been developed that can crack highly sophisticated encryption schemes that do much more than merely shift letters by a fixed number of positions.

The ability to use software to crack encryption schemes poses an ongoing challenge for professional cryptographers. It is highly desirable and in many cases necessary to encrypt sensitive information such as medical records, financial data, and military intelligence, yet in theory, someone who is able to obtain a copy of such information could use a computer to try out all possible decryption schemes on the encrypted information until the computer finds the right "key" to the information that has been encrypted. The two primary ways in which encryption can be used to protect against such attacks are (1) to encrypt sensitive information using a scheme that is so complicated that decrypting the information would take months or years even using today's most powerful computers in an attempt to crack the code, and (2) to change the encryption applied to sensitive information frequently enough—such as every week or every month—so that by the time an eavesdropper figured out how to crack the original encryption scheme, it would already have been changed. This "cat and mouse" game between cryptographers and people who try to hack into encrypted information is what will keep skilled professional cryptographers in high demand for a very long time.

CRYPTOGRAPHY IN THE ANCIENT WORLD

Examples of ancient cryptography that have survived show the use of two basic encryption operations that are still employed today: permutation and substitution of characters. In the fifth century B.C.E., the Spartans of ancient Greece used a tool called a *scytale* to encrypt messages using character permutation. The scytale was a stick with a fixed diameter. For encryption, a narrow strip of parchment was wound around the scytale, and the message was written on it. When the parchment was removed from the scytale, it displayed a sequence of letters that were meaningless to anyone who tried to read them. The receiver would decrypt the message by winding the parchment around a scytale with the same diameter to reveal the meaning of the letters. This is known as a permutation cipher because the original letters are used and only their order is changed.

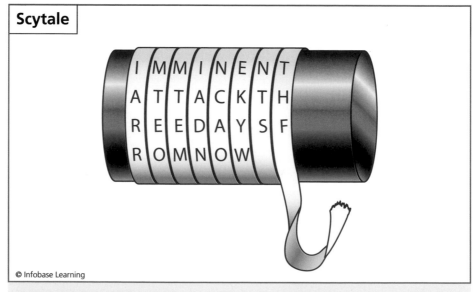

Scytale

© Infobase Learning

Ancient Greeks used the scytale to encrypt and decrypt messages written on parchment and delivered over long distances.

The ancient Roman army used a substitution encryption method known as the Caesar shift cipher. Each letter in the message was substituted with the letter three positions away in the alphabet. For example, A would become D, C would become F, and so on. The message was decrypted by reversing the substitution. For a substitution encryption method such as the Caesar shift, the number of positions away can be varied each time a message is encrypted. Knowing how many positions were shifted is known as the key to the encryption. The Caesar cipher is an example of "symmetric-key encryption," because the same key is used for both encryption and decryption.

The Renaissance architect Leon Battista Alberti (1404–72) invented a device that assisted with the encryption and decryption of the Caesar cipher. The device consisted of two concentric rotating discs. When the disks were rotated by the correct number of positions, the encrypted letters lined up. In recognition of this and other work, Alberti is often referred to as the "father of Western cryptography."

CRYPTOGRAPHY IN WORLD WAR II

Following World War I, an electromechanical machine that could effectively encrypt and decrypt secret messages was invented by the German engineer Arthur Scherbius (1878–1929). This was the Enigma machine (see the sidebar on pages 19–20), used for commercial applications in the 1920s and then adapted for military and government use by several countries. Various models of the machine were developed, but the version known as the Werhmacht Enigma is the most famous due to its use by Nazi Germany during World War II and the challenge it presented to Allied forces to crack its code.

One of the most important elements in the encryption of a message by the Enigma was the setup of its initial state, known as the cryptographic key. The key was determined by several variables, including the configuration of the rotors, the position of an alphabet ring, and the settings of a plugboard that performed alphabetic substitution before encryption by the rotor mechanism. In order to decipher a message, one needed both a description of the cryptographic key and the same model of Enigma machine as the one that was used to encrypt the message. This high degree of complexity made encrypted messages generated using the Enigma extremely difficult to crack.

The Enigma was used by Germany in World War II to encrypt messages for transmission throughout Europe. *(National Security Agency)*

The Enigma and Bombe machines are important parts of the history of cryptography for several reasons. They were the most sophisticated machines up until that point to be used for message encryption and decryption. Alan Turing would go on to become one of the founders of the field of computer science. He developed many of the central concepts of computation, computer design, programming, and artificial intelligence. Finally, the Bombe played a key role in the events of World War II. It gave the Allied forces the ability to secretly decipher Enigma-encoded messages, leading to the defeat of the German U-Boat offensive in the Atlantic. Many lives were saved by the decryption capabilities provided by the Bombe.

THE PROBLEM WITH SHARED KEYS: THE MAN-IN-THE-MIDDLE ATTACK

In the field of cryptography, eavesdropping or intercepting encrypted messages is referred to as an attack. The act of eavesdropping is known as a passive attack, while the act of intercepting a message, modifying it, and then forwarding it is known as an active attack. The man-in-the-middle attack is the most common form of active attack and involves a third party who intercepts messages in an exchange between two parties. The two parties believe they are communicating with each other when they are actually communicating with the attacker. The man-in-the-middle attack (abbreviated MITM) is also known as a bucket-brigade attack or Janus attack.

For simple *shared key* encryption schemes such as the Caesar cipher, in which a single key is shared by both the sender and receiver of an encrypted message, one of the most persistent problems is how the sender can provide the shared key to the receiver without the shared key being intercepted by an eavesdropper. The use of a shared key makes it easier for MITM attacks to occur, especially when the sender and receiver of a message are in different locations. In this case, the key must be transmitted securely, and the risks of the key being intercepted are great. Once the key is known by a third party, that party can read, modify, and retransmit encrypted messages without the knowledge of the sender or receiver.

THE SOLUTION: PUBLIC-KEY CRYPTOGRAPHY

As described in the previous section, the use of a shared key leaves an encryption scheme vulnerable to an active attack. The fundamental problem with a shared key is how to make the key known to both parties without it being intercepted.

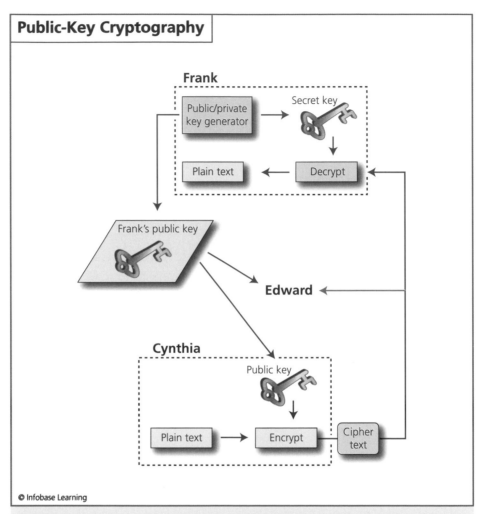

Public-Key Cryptography

Public-key cryptography enables people to send and receive encrypted messages without the need to transmit their secret encryption keys over insecure channels. For Cynthia to send an encrypted message to Frank, she need only use Frank's public key to encrypt the message and then send the encrypted message ("cipher text") to Frank. Edward's access to Frank's public key does not enable Edward to decrypt the encrypted message. Only Frank, the sole possessor of Frank's secret key, can decrypt the encrypted message using his secret key.

To address this problem, the concept of *public-key encryption* was developed by two American cryptologists, Whitfield Diffie and Martin Hellman, in 1975.

A public-key cryptographic system is "asymmetric," in contrast to symmetric shared-key systems. In a public key cryptographic system, a pair of keys, rather than a single shared key, is used to perform encryption and decryption. Each party who wants to send and receive encrypted messages needs to first generate a public key and a *private key* for himself or herself. Software exists for generating such keys. People then make their public keys available to the public, such as by posting them on a Web site or in a "registry" of public keys. Now, assume that two parties, A and B, each have generated public and private keys for themselves and that A wants to transmit an encrypted message to B. To do so, A first obtains B's public key. Next, A encrypts the message using B's public key and transmits the encrypted message to B. An eavesdropper who has also

Using Public-Key Cryptography for Digital Signatures

One of the most important benefits of public-key cryptography is that it enables support for digital signatures. A digital signature allows the recipient of a message to verify that the origin of the message is authentic and that all parts of the message are intact. This means that information can be authenticated and its integrity validated. Additionally, a digital signature prevents the sender from claiming the message was sent from someone else. This is known as a nonrepudiation capability.

A digital signature can be compared to a handwritten signature, with the added benefit that it is almost impossible to forge. Above and beyond a handwritten signature, the digital signature also stands as proof that the information is valid and the signature authentic.

Digital signatures use public-key cryptography in a slightly different way. The private key is used for encryption and the public key for decryption. An additional component that makes the digital signature even more secure is the *digital certificate*. Since anyone could create public and private keys and attempt to use them with someone else's digital signature, thereby launching a man-in-the-middle attack, a digital certificate is used to establish the identity of the holder of a digital signature. A digital certificate contains identifying information related to the owner of a public key and digital signature. Software such as Web browsers use digital certificates to verify that the sender of an electronic message is who the digital signature says it is.

obtained B's public key cannot use that key to decrypt the message. When B receives the encrypted message, B uses his or her private key—which has been kept secret—to decrypt the message.

Since B's public key can be used only to encrypt messages intended for B but not to decrypt such messages, and since only B's private key (which B has kept secret) can be used to decrypt messages that have been encrypted using B's public key, this system is much more secure against man-in-the-middle attacks than are shared-key systems. As a result, the development of public-key cryptography systems marked a revolutionary change in cryptography, allowing messages to be securely encrypted without incurring the additional expense of using secure methods to relay a shared key. Instead, parties can transmit their public keys to each other using insecure methods, such as e-mail, without fear of comprising the secrecy of their encrypted messages.

CRYPTOGRAPHY IN EVERYDAY LIFE

In the modern world, cryptography has moved beyond secret messages and ciphers. Governments, financial institutions, and large companies require encryption of massive amounts of sensitive data. With recent growth in the use of the Internet, increasingly sophisticated encryption and decryption systems have been developed. Modern cryptography uses mathematics and information systems for the creation of ever more secure encryption methods.

Authentication and digital signatures are part of everyday life, even when we are not aware that they are at work. Online shopping and banking, credit cards, mobile phones—these are just a few examples of areas that use modern cryptography and digital signatures. The storage and exchange of medical information in electronic form is another application that requires highly secure encryption and decryption techniques.

Digital signatures and certificates are a key element on e-commerce Web sites. The security of credit card numbers, passwords, and bank transactions is guaranteed through standard cryptographic protocols, digital signatures, and digital certificates. Digital signatures are used for digital rights management, a technique used by music publishers to limit the distribution of digital music files. Digital signatures are also used with Adobe's Portable Document Format (PDF) to serve as legal signatures on business contracts and other important documents.

CHALLENGES IN CRYPTOGRAPHY TODAY

The challenges facing cryptology today revolve around the fundamental issues of cost, speed, and long-term security. With increasing amounts of information being stored on distributed devices, including cell phones, smart cards, and flash drives as well as computers and network servers, there is a need to keep the cost of encryption low and the speed high. As smaller devices gain more memory for data storage, there is great demand for high-speed encryption with low energy requirements implemented at the hardware level.

The difficulty of cracking an encrypted message increases exponentially as the length of the encryption key that was used to encrypt the message increases. This means that for every bit (0 or 1 in binary) that is added to an encryption key, messages encrypted with that key become twice as difficult to decrypt. For example, a message encrypted with a 64-bit encryption key is twice as difficult to crack as a message encrypted with a 63-bit encryption key. Cracking a message encrypted with a 64-bit key using a brute force attack, which tries all possible combinations of encryption keys, would, on average, require trying half of all possible 64-bit keys (see table).

The minimum key length needed to provide sufficient security depends on the situation. Today, it is generally agreed that when using public key cryptography, a minimum key length of 2048 bits is needed for adequate security in most

(continues on page 46)

STRENGTH OF CRYPTOGRAPHIC KEYS OF VARYING LENGTHS	
Length of Key	Number of Possible Keys
8	256
64	1.844×10^{19} (~184,467,441,000,000)
128	3.402×10^{38} (~340,282,367,000,000,000,000,000,000,000,000,000,000)
256	1.157×10^{77} (~115,792,089,000,000,000,000,000,000,000,000,000,000,000,000, 000,000,000,000,000,000,000,000,000,000,000)
1,024	179,769,313 followed by 300 zeros
2,048	323,170,060 followed by 608 zeros
3,072	580,960,599 followed by 916 zeros

0011010100101001110101101010101011001010000 1

Rivest, Shamir, and Adleman: Inventors of RSA Encryption Algorithm

Ronald Rivest, Adi Shamir, and Leonard Adleman are the inventors of the RSA cryptoalgorithm, the most widely used public-key cryptography system today. Rivest, Shamir, and Adleman received the prestigious ACM Turing Award in 2002, which is often called the Nobel Prize of computer science, for their work on the cryptoalgorithm as well as the 2000 IEEE Koji Kobayashi Computers and Communications award and the Secure Computing Lifetime Achievement Award. Today, the RSA system is used in secure Web browsers, e-mail systems, virtual private networks, digital signatures, mobile phones, and a variety of other applications that require a secure transfer of information.

Created in 1977, the cryptoalgorithm works by selecting two prime numbers, each of which is usually at least 100 bits long, and multiplying them to yield an encryption key. This key is then plugged into the RSA algorithm to encrypt the message. The algorithm works because even the most prominent mathematicians have been unable to find a way to quickly factor large integers; factoring an integer requires finding the prime numbers that are multiplied together to yield the integer. The encryption key can be passed along or posted on the Internet because the algorithm requires that the recipient know both integers in order to decrypt the message. Therefore, a secret message sent using RSA encryption yields a code that is impossible to decipher with just the encryption key itself. One must know the original numbers that went into creating it. For example, if Jane wants to send a secret message to John, she asks John to provide her with an encryption key. John chooses the two integers and sends Jane the resulting product. Jane then writes the message and enters the key into the algorithm. She can then send the resulting encrypted code back to John, who decrypts it using the original integers. Even though others can see the encrypted message and the public key, due to the difficulty in factoring large integers, it is nearly impossible for someone else to guess the prime integers correctly.

Leonard Adleman is a theoretical computer scientist. He is currently a professor of computer science and molecular biology at the University of Southern California. Born in 1945, Adleman received his bachelor's degree in mathemat-

0011010100101001110101101010101011001010000 1

1001110100101010100110010111011010100101001

ics in 1968 as well as a Ph.D. in electrical engineering and computer science from the University of California at Berkeley. Aside from his participation in the development of RSA, Adleman's contributions to computer science include the first known successful instance of using DNA to compute an algorithm, detailed in his 1994 paper "Molecular Computations of Solutions to Combinatorial Problems." DNA computations work by synthesizing a mixture of DNA strands to logically represent the problem's solution space. Biochemical tech-

Adi Shamir (the "S" in RSA encryption) speaks about encryption at a conference in 2007. *(Gabriel Bouys/AFP/Getty Images)*

niques are then used to algorithmically operate on the space and weed out the incorrect strands, leaving only the strands that could satisfy the problem, or in other words, just the possible solutions. Analyzing the nucleotide sequence of these strands reveals the correct solutions to the problem. DNA computing thus can be used to solve large-scale combinatorial search problems. In 2002, Adleman and his research team were able use DNA computation to solve a 20-variable 3-SAT problem that had more than a million potential solutions.

Adleman is one of the discoverers of the Adleman Pomerance Rumely primality test. He was the mathematical consultant for the 1992 movie *Sneakers* and is also an amateur boxer.

Adi Shamir was born in Tel Aviv, Israel, in 1952. He received a bachelor's degree in mathematics from Tel Aviv University in 1973 and a Ph.D. in computer science from the Weizmann Institute in 1977. Following a year at the University of Warwick, Shamir spent three years at MIT doing research. He returned to the Weizmann Institute to teach mathematics and computer science in 1980. Since 2006, he has taught at the Ecole Normale Superieure in Paris.

(continues)

1001110100101010100110010111011010100101001

(continued)

Shamir's contributions to cryptography, in addition to his involvement with the development of RSA, include visual cryptography, the breaking of the Merkle-Hellman cryptosystem, and the Shamir secret sharing scheme. Together with Eli Biham, Shamir discovered differential cryptanalysis, a general method for attacking block ciphers, which, as it turned out, was already being used by the NSA and kept secret.

In addition to the Turing Award for his work on the RSA algorithm, Shamir is the recipient of the CM's Kannelakis Award, the Vatican's PIUS XI Gold Medal, the IEEE Koji Kobayashi Computers and Communications Award, and the Israel Prize for computer sciences in 2008.

Ronald Rivest received a bachelor's degree in mathematics from Yale University in 1969, a Ph.D. in computer science from Stanford University in 1974, and an honorary degree from the University of Rome. He is the Viterbi Professor of Computer Science at MIT. He is also a member of the MIT Computer Science and Artificial Intelligence Laboratory, a part of the Theory of Computation Group within the lab, and the leader of the Cryptography and Information Security Group. Recognized as an authority in the field of cryptography, Rivest has published numerous papers on cryptanalysis and cryptographic design. He has done extensive work on computer algorithms and machine learning. He is the founder of RSA Data Security, cofounder of the digital signature company Verisign, and cofounder of the cryptography company Peppercoin.

(continued from page 43)

situations. However, as computers become more powerful, it will become necessary to use increasingly longer keys. For example, RSA Corporation claims that although 2048-bit keys should be sufficient until the year 2030, those seeking to create messages that will remain uncrackable even after 2030 should use keys that are at least 3072 bits long. Organizations such as the International Association of Cryptologic Research are working to identify additional cryptography challenges and are developing new cryptographic algorithms and ciphers for use in the future.

CONCLUSIONS

The human desire and need for secrecy has led to the use of cryptography for almost as long as people have transmitted messages to one another. Cryptography was probably used even before written language existed, as is evidenced today by native speakers of a foreign language who speak to each other in a crowded room in their native tongue in an attempt to keep their conversation secret from others in the room who do not speak the same language. It can be critical to encrypt even very short messages when failure to keep the contents of such messages can cause significant harm, as in the case of generals communicating troop movements to each other. Today, effective cryptography is important for the average person both because sensitive data about individuals, such as financial and medical histories, are increasingly being stored on computers that are accessible over the Internet and because the sheer amount of data stored and transmitted by and on behalf of everyday people continues to increase exponentially, thereby increasing the likelihood that even a single breach of encryption at an institution such as a bank, hospital, or Internet service provider will result in a significant compromise of the privacy and security of a large number of people.

The typical home computer user would like for all of his or her private data to be encrypted both completely automatically and with perfect security, yet it is not possible in practice to achieve these goals. As described above, all encryption systems use a key to decrypt messages. Although efforts can be made to make such keys difficult for third parties to guess, it is always possible that someone who tries a large enough number of possible keys will eventually find the key necessary to decrypt a particular set of encrypted data. Someone with access to a powerful computer can try a large number of keys very quickly. As computers grow increasingly powerful and as it becomes possible to combine the power of an increasingly large number of networked computers, it is becoming possible to try a larger and larger number of keys in shorter and shorter amounts of time. Although one way to counteract such efforts is to make keys longer and therefore less likely to be guessed, even this approach can be foiled by yet more powerful computers.

In practice, the most powerful tool that the average computer user has in protecting his or her own data against being decrypted is to choose his own key, usually in the form of a password, in a way that makes it difficult to guess, to change such keys frequently (such as every month), and to store such keys in very secure places. Although this requires more effort and time than letting one's bank or Internet service provider choose one's key automatically, the need for extra time is offset by an increase in security. As long as the cat-and-mouse game continues between cryptographers and those who seek to access other people's private data, there will be no other option than for people to take some degree of personal responsibility for keeping their own data safe and secure.

4

MATHEMATICAL PROOFS: COMPUTERS FIND TRUTH

The concept of a proof is one of the features that distinguishes mathematics from other sciences. A mathematical proof is the demonstration that a conclusion is true by following a chain of logic based on a set of established rules. This method of proving a conclusion is known as deductive reasoning. The conclusion that a mathematical proof addresses is referred to as a theorem. When deductive reasoning is used for a mathematical proof, it must show that the theorem is true in all cases and that no exceptions can be found. Examples of theorems include statements such as "the base angles of an isosceles triangle are equal to each other" and "the square root of 2 is an irrational number."

In contrast, the natural sciences use inductive reasoning, which cannot produce conclusions that can be demonstrated to be true with complete certainty and under all circumstances. In inductive reasoning, a particular event is observed to occur a certain number of times, such as the Sun rising in the morning every day for a year. The process of induction is then used to conclude that the same event will occur again under the same circumstances in the future—the Sun will rise again tomorrow morning. Although such inductive reasoning can produce conclusions that are relatively likely to be true, they cannot be proved to be true with the certainty of a mathematical theorem produced using deductive reasoning. For example, if the Earth were to spin out of its orbit, the Sun might not rise again the next morning.

The use of proofs in mathematics dates back to early Greek civilization. The mathematical discoveries of the Greeks and of every major mathematician since then have a timeless quality due to the use of rigorous proofs. The word *rigorous* is often applied to the description of a mathematical proof. This means that the proof strictly follows a set of established rules and procedures. One of the procedures for proving a mathematical theorem is to base the proof on statements that are accepted as true without proof. This is known as a derived proof. Such an accepted but unproven true statement used in a derived proof is called an *axiom*.

A derived mathematical proof usually begins with a theorem, a set of axioms (also known as assumptions), and a set of definitions and then follows logical steps to draw conclusions from the axioms and definitions until eventually the theorem is proven true. Intermediate statements that are proven to be true on the way to proving the final theorem are known as *lemmas*. Logical arguments are applied to lemmas, and inferences are drawn using such arguments to arrive at the conclusion that the theorem is true.

To see this process at work, take the example of the theorem "the base angles of an isosceles triangle are equal to each other." Picture a triangle with two sides of equal length, known as "congruent" sides with a line extending from the top vertex to the base. This line is perpendicular to the base (meaning that the line forms right angles with the base). By visually inspecting the triangle, it is obvious that the two base vertex angles are congruent. A protractor can be used to measure the angles and confirm that they are equal. How can the premise that these angles are equal be extended to refer to *every possible* isosceles triangle? How many triangles would have to be measured—50, 100, 1,000? The goal of a mathematical proof is to demonstrate beyond doubt that a mathematical statement is true in all cases without requiring each case to be individually verified.

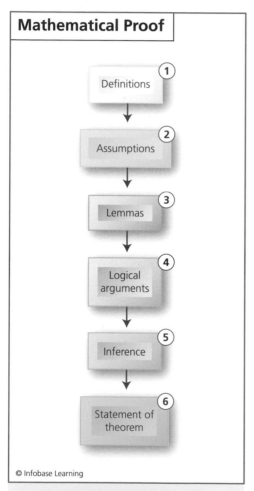

Mathematical Proof

1. Definitions
2. Assumptions
3. Lemmas
4. Logical arguments
5. Inference
6. Statement of theorem

© Infobase Learning

A mathematical proof demonstrates the truth of a mathematical statement by proceeding methodically from definitions (axioms) to a proven theorem.

TYPES OF MATHEMATICAL PROOFS

Although all mathematical proofs proceed using axioms and definitions, proofs take many forms involving many kinds of logic. The following is a list of a few examples of the kinds of proofs used by mathematicians to prove theorems.

- *Direct proof*

  In a direct proof, a theorem is proven true or false by combining definitions, axioms, and previously proven theorems.

- *Proof by Contradiction*

  For a proof by contradiction, the goal is to show that if a given statement is true, then a contradiction exists. Therefore, the given statement cannot be true. This is one of the easiest and most commonly used methods of proof.

- *Existence Proof*

  To prove that something with a given set of properties exists, finding an instance can be a sufficient proof. For example, the number 2 proves that a prime number can be even, because 2 is an instance of a prime number that is even.

- *Proof by Mathematical Induction*

  This method of proof works from a series of cases. The theorem is shown to be true for a base case. A rule of induction is then used to prove a series of other cases. This method of proof is often used with the set of all natural numbers. If the statement is true for one number, it will also be true for the next number and for all numbers stretching to infinity.

- *Proof by Exhaustion*

  This method is sometimes referred to as a brute force proof. For this method, a statement is proved by creating a large number of finite cases, each of which is proved individually. The first step in this method is to prove that the cases used are exhaustive, and the second step is the proof of each case. There is no rule on how many cases must be proved for proof by exhaustion. Because the number of cases may be very large, computers are often used to assist in checking the validity of each case.

001101010010100111010110101010101011001010000 1

Proof: The Square Root of 2 Is an Irrational Number

The easiest way to understand how a mathematical proof works is to see one "in action." The following is an explanation of one proof that the square root of the number 2 is an "irrational" number. To understand the proof, it is useful first to understand what an irrational number is.

A "rational" number is a number that can be written as a fraction in which both the number on the top of the fraction (the "numerator") and the number on the bottom of the fraction (the "denominator") are whole numbers ("integers"). For example, 0.75 is a rational number because it can be written as the fraction 3/4, in which both the numerator and the denominator are whole numbers. The same is true of numbers such as 0.8 (4/5), 1.9 (19/10), and 10 (10/1).

Some numbers contain an infinite number of digits after the decimal point. For example, the number "one-third" is written as a decimal as $0.333\bar{3}$ where the horizontal line over the final 3 indicates that there are an infinite number of 3s after the decimal point. Some such numbers are still rational numbers because they can be written as a fraction in which the numerator and denominator are whole numbers. In this example, $0.333\bar{3}$ is a rational number because it can be written as the fraction 1/3.

Not all numbers with an infinite number of digits after the decimal point are rational numbers, however. For example, the number π (pronounced "pie"), which is the ratio of the circumference of a circle to its diameter, is written as the number 3.14159 . . . and is an irrational number because it is not possible to write it as a fraction with integers as numerator and denominator. For example, the fraction 7/22 is close but not exactly equal to π.

The same is true of the square root of 2 (the number which, when multiplied by itself, is equal to 2). Although a calculator may indicate that the square root of 2 is roughly equal to 1.41421, this is only an approximation. The exact value of the square root of 2 has an infinite number of digits after the decimal point. Although one might be able to look at the square root of 2 and *guess* that it is an irrational number, such a hunch is not a proof. Even writing down millions of different fractions and demonstrating that none of them was equal to the square root of 2 would still not prove no *other* fraction is equal to the square root of 2. One cannot, in other words, prove the irrationality of the square root of 2 by brute force alone.

Many proofs that the square root of 2 is an irrational number have been produced over hundreds of years. The following is one of the easiest to understand

001101010010100111010110101010101011001010000 1

10011101001010101001100101110110101001010 01

but still requires some concentration to follow. It may need to be read a few times to digest it completely.

If the square root of 2 (written as $\sqrt{2}$) were a *rational* number, it would be possible to write it as a fraction a/b such that both a and b are whole numbers. Assume that a and b have been reduced to their smallest possible values. For example, if one were to start out with $a = 4$ and $b = 8$, this would yield the fraction 4/8, which can be reduced to 1/2 but no further because it is not possible to divide both a and b by the same number while maintaining both a and b as whole numbers. In this case, $a = 1$ and $b = 2$.

If $\sqrt{2} = a/b$, then by squaring both sides of the equation, we know that $2 = a^2/b^2$. Multiplying both sides of the equation by b^2 tells us that $a^2 = 2b^2$. This tells us that a^2 is equal to 2 times b^2, which tells us that a^2 is an even number (any number that is equal to 2 times another number is an even number). From this we can deduce that a itself is also an even number, because only the squares of even numbers are also even numbers. (Try multiplying any odd number by itself and you will see that the squares of odd numbers are always odd numbers.)

Since a is an even number, we know that $a = 2c$, where c is some other number. If we substitute $a = 2c$ into the original equation $2 = a^2/b^2$, we get $2 = (2c)^2/b^2$, which in turn yields $2 = 4c^2/b^2$ because $(2c)^2 = 4c^2$. Multiplying both sides of this equation by b^2 yields $2b^2 = 4c^2$. Dividing both sides of the equation by 2 tells us that $b^2 = 2c^2$. We can deduce from this that b^2 is an even number (because it is equal to 2 times another number) and therefore that b itself is an even number.

We have now deduced that both a and b are even numbers. But if they are both even numbers, then the fraction a/b is not reduced to its lowest terms. For example, if a is the even number 4 and b is the even number 8, then the fraction $a/b = 4/8$. This is not reduced to its lowest terms because 4/8 can be further reduced to 1/2. The same is true if a and b are *any* even numbers.

The original assumption made at the beginning of the proof—that the fraction a/b has been reduced to its lowest terms—lead to the conclusion that the fraction a/b has *not* been reduced to its lowest terms. This is a logical contradiction. Therefore, the premise that there is a fraction a/b such that both a and b are integers and for which $\sqrt{2} = a/b$ cannot be true. Since $\sqrt{2}$ cannot be written as such a fraction, $\sqrt{2}$ cannot be rational—it must be irrational.

10011101001010101001100101110110101001010 01

WHAT IS A COMPUTER-ASSISTED PROOF?

A computer-assisted mathematical proof relies on data that are computer generated. Computer-assisted proofs often are used for theorems that are well suited to proof by the exhaustion method and involve a large number of cases. To perform a computer-assisted proof, a mathematician creates a computer program, called a *theorem prover*, that performs the computations needed to prove the theorem. The mathematician provides the individual cases as input to the computer, in response to which the computer completes the calculations. In one sense, the computer acts as a high-speed, highly accurate calculating assistant to the mathematician to perform the calculations necessary to prove each case for which proof is needed.

Among mathematicians, computer-assisted proofs have had a controversial history because such proofs derive their strength from acceptance of the results of computations rather than on agreement with a chain of logic constructed from definitions, axioms, and proven theorems. Mathematicians who dislike computer-assisted proofs prefer those that consist of short, general statements connected by logic rather than pages full of the results of thousands of complex calculations performed by a computer. Some mathematicians also argue that computer-assisted proofs that require more cases than can be verified by a human are not authentic. On the other hand, mathematicians who support computer-assisted proofs contend that while such proofs may include computations that are performed by machines, the computer program that defines the computations must be created by a mathematician and verified by other mathematicians, thereby making the conclusions drawn from such proofs legitimate.

The "four-color theorem" was the first major theorem to be proven using a computer-assisted proof. This theorem states that given an area that has been completely divided into regions (such as a map of the continental United States), the regions can be individually colored by using at most four colors so that no two adjacent regions have the same color. The definition of "adjacent" for purposes of this theorem is that two regions are adjacent when they share a side border. If one draws random maps and tries to color them with as few colors as possible, it eventually becomes clear that such maps always can be colored using at most four colors. The challenge, however, is to prove beyond any doubt that this is true for all possible maps.

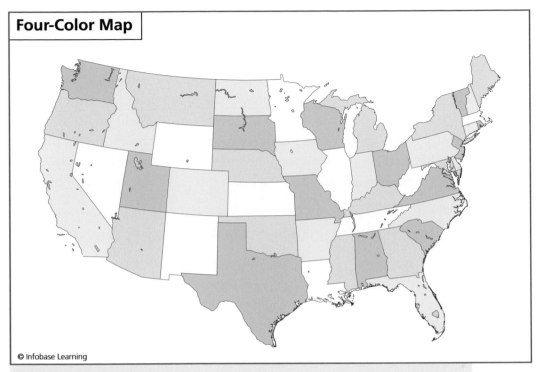

Four-Color Map

© Infobase Learning

It was long assumed but not proven that any map, such as this map of the contiguous United States, could be colored with no more than four colors without coloring any two adjacent regions with the same color. (The choice of the colors themselves is arbitrary and does not carry any meaning.) This so-called four-color theorem eventually was proved with the assistance of a computer.

A computer was first used to prove the four-color theorem by Kenneth Appel and Wolfgang Haken in 1976. Their proof used a set of 1,936 maps to check that each map satisfied the requirements of the theorem. Appel and Haken wrote the computer program that verified that each map satisfied the theorem. They also completed analysis by hand that proved that any other map must have a portion that resembled one of the 1,936 maps. This analysis included proof that no maps could be found that are counterexamples of the theorem. When Appel and Haken introduced their proof, there was doubt among mathematicians about its validity. Many of those doubts continue to this day. In addition to the large volume of computer data used in the proof, the analysis done by hand is extremely complex and has never been officially verified.

In 1997, a simpler computer-assisted proof for the four-color theorem was published by Neil Robertson, Daniel Sander, Paul Seymour, and Robin Thomas. In 2005, Georges Gonthier used general-purpose proof software to prove the four-color theorem. This general-purpose software represents the next phase in computer-assisted proofs and draws upon techniques such as heuristic search that have come from research in the field of artificial intelligence. Proofs created with general-purpose proof software are not disputed so widely as those that use computer assistance for computations used in the proof by exhaustion method.

BENEFITS OF COMPUTER-ASSISTED PROOFS

The most obvious benefit of a computer-assisted proof is that it uses a reliable tool for verification of test cases. Computations performed by computer are known to be highly accurate, and the program that is used to generate the computations can in most cases be verified by a human. When the scope of the proof makes sense for computer assistance and when the arguments and algorithms used for the proof are clearly presented and explained, a computer-assisted proof is completely acceptable in the eyes of many mathematicians. The proof of the four-color theorem that was developed by Robertson, Sanders, Seymour, and Thomas is often used as an example of a computer-assisted proof that was very well presented. The explanation is about 18 pages in length, and all the test case maps that are used are generated by computer code rather than fed in as input (a tedious and possibly error-prone process). Mathematicians who favor computer-assisted proofs believe that computers are useful tools that may lead the way to new discoveries in mathematics and related fields and that computer-assisted proofs can help make mathematics accessible to a wider audience.

OBJECTIONS TO COMPUTER-ASSISTED PROOFS

When computer-assisted proofs are lengthy and complex, some mathematicians believe they are not authentic proofs since they cannot be practically verified by a human being. They distrust proofs that require faith in a computational process rather than in logical deductions based on established axioms.

The process of programming a computer to assist in a proof is prone to error from a variety of sources, including the source code, the compiler used on the source code, and the hardware on which the program runs. For many mathematicians, the possibility of error in the calculations of a computer-assisted proof is too great. Another criticism of computer-assisted proofs is that they lack mathematical elegance and provide nothing that will spark new insights and ideas. For those who are interested in the philosophical side of mathematics, computer-assisted proofs are often seen as removing logic and reasoning from mathematics in favor of symbol manipulation.

ROLE OF MATHEMATICIANS IN COMPUTER-ASSISTED PROOFS

The evolution of computer-assisted proofs is beginning to challenge the role of the mathematician. In the past, the purpose of a mathematical proof was to allow one mathematician to convince others of the validity of a statement. The elegance of the mathematician's logic was essential to the proof. The process was often collaborative, involving contributions from a group of mathematicians.

When computers are used to construct proofs, the results are often hard to understand and must be accepted as true since they have been computed. Rather than elegant logic, a computer-assisted proof relies on the accuracy of the data it produces. Many see the mathematician who uses a computer to assist in proofs as less of a philosopher and more of an experimenter, using the computer as a tool to create data that support a proof.

Computer scientists are in the habit of creating verification software to check the validity of their own programs. Mathematicians who work with computer-assisted proofs now find themselves following the lead of computer scientists and creating software that checks the validity of computer-assisted mathematical proofs. As computer-assisted proofs become more widely used, the definitions of what constitutes a good proof may begin to change, and the process of creating an accepted proof will involve collaboration between mathematicians and machines rather than groups of mathematicians.

Kenneth Appel and Wolfgang Haken: Mathematicians Who Used Computer Software to Prove the "Four-Color Theorem"

Kenneth Appel was born in 1932 and studied at Queens College and the University of Michigan. He did research at the Institute for Defense Analysis at Princeton University before joining the faculty of the University of Illinois at Urbana-Champaign in 1961. Together with Wolfgang Haken, his colleague at the University of Illinois, Appel solved one of the most famous mathematical problems, thereby proving the "four-color theorem."

The four-color theorem, also known as the four-color map problem, was an 1852 postulation by Francis Guthrie, who sought to prove that four colors are always sufficient to color neighboring countries on a two-dimensional map with different colors so that no adjacent countries are the same color. The problem was presented to the London Mathematical Society in 1878, and less than a year later, Alfred Bray Kempe published a paper that attempted to show that Guthrie's conclusion was correct. However, soon a significant flaw was discovered by Percy John Heawood, and work on the four-color theorem continued until it was finally proved true in 1976 by Appel and Haken.

Unlike their predecessors, Appel and Haken's four-year quest relied heavily on the use of computers for calculations and sorting through possible answers. It

CONCLUSIONS

The word *proof* has a different meaning in everyday speech than it does in mathematics. People speak of having "proved" that a new weight loss pill is effective after testing it on a few hundred people, having "proved" that a signature was forged based on handwriting analysis, and having "proved" that a tax increase has stimulated the economy after observing improved economic conditions. Although such uses of *prove* are not necessarily objectionable, they are not intended to imply that their conclusions have been demonstrated to be true beyond all doubt. A "proven" weight loss pill might not cause certain people to lose weight, just as it is possible that a signature that has been "proven" to be forged may in fact have been written by the person whose name it represents. In

10011101001010101001100101110110101001 01001

was one of the first times that computers were used not just as engineering tools but as a way to aid mathematical theory research.

After leaving Urbana-Champaign, Appel headed the department of mathematics at the University of New Hampshire in Durham from 1993 to 2002. Now retired, he still occasionally teaches there and continues to work.

In addition to his work on the four-color theorem, Haken is a respected figure in the field of algorithmic topology. He introduced the idea of Haken manifolds. He also developed an algorithm that can detect whether a knot is topologically equivalent to an unknotted circle, known as the "unknot."

Kenneth Appel (pictured) and Wolfgang Haken used a computer to prove the four-color theorem in 1976. *(Doug Prince/University of New Hampshire Photographic Services)*

10011101001010101001100101110110101001 01001

mathematics, however, *proven* has a different, more rigorous meaning. A mathematical theorem is considered to be "proven" only when it has been demonstrated to be true in all circumstances and without any doubt.

It might seem at first glance that the rigorous standard that must be satisfied by mathematical proofs does not have any applicability to the real world. In most circumstances that people encounter, a conclusion that has been proven to be true with 99.99 percent certainty can be relied upon for all practical purposes, even if there is a remaining .01 percent likelihood that the conclusion is false. Absolute certainty is not required. The fact that the Sun has risen in the morning and set in the evening for every day of human history can reliably serve as the basis for the conclusion that the Sun will rise again for every day of the remainder of human history, even though modern science predicts that at some point, probably several billion years in the future, the Sun will burn out and therefore stop rising. Given the ability of nonabsolute proofs to guide us reliably through our lives, one might wonder what value the methods of mathematical proofs and the absolute conclusions they draw have in human affairs.

One benefit of mathematical proofs is that learning how to prove mathematical theorems provides excellent training in rigorous logical thinking. Proving that a particular mathematical statement is true requires

- identifying with complete clarity the premises (axioms) that are to be used as a starting point;
- defining the rules that are allowed to be used in drawing conclusions from those premises; and
- following the defined rules exactly, without making any logical leaps that are not justified by the rules and without drawing conclusions based on emotion or preconceived notions about whether the desired conclusion is correct.

All of these skills are useful in any context in which critical thinking is required. Just in the public policy arena alone, decisions about how to raise and distribute money from taxes; how to punish and rehabilitate criminals; and what the government's role should be in fields such as health care, education, and banking would all benefit from a healthy dose of rational, evidence-based thinking that starts from assumptions that everyone agrees on and which proceeds according to rules of logic that everyone agrees to follow. Even though emotion, personal preferences, and less savory qualities such as greed inevitably factor into such decisions, if the kinds of critical thinking skills associated with mathematical proofs were more widespread, more people would be able to recognize attempts to use faulty logic to influence public decisions and thereby avoid being manipulated.

The methods of mathematical proof are even more directly applicable to the design of safe and reliable products and facilities. One of the most difficult tasks faced by an engineer when designing any new product is to predict how the product will behave under a wide variety of conditions. It is easy enough to test a new lawn mower for safety by using it to mow a flat, neatly manicured lawn. However, to ensure that the lawn mower is safe for sale to the general public, it should be tested on bumpy lawns, on lawns covered with rocks and sticks, and in both extreme heat and extreme cold because consumers will probably use the mower under these kinds of conditions and because it can be very difficult to predict whether the mower will fly apart or do something else dangerous under various conditions without actually testing the mower under such conditions. Even more difficult from the perspective of the lawn mower designer is predicting and testing the full range of conditions under which any consumer might reasonably use the lawn mower. For example, mowing after a heavy rain might cause the mower to roll through deep puddles of water. Failure to test the mower in this way, or at least failure to warn consumers *not* to use the mower in this way, could lead to a malfunction that causes damage to the mower or, worse yet, injury to its owner.

The need to verify the proper operation of engineered systems is even more important when the system

- includes a very large number of parts that interact with one another in complex ways, such as automobiles, wastewater treatment plants, and computers;
- could cause serious injury to a large number of people upon a malfunction, as is the case with nuclear power plants, airplanes, and military weapons, and
- cannot be repaired easily in case of a malfunction, as is the case with helicopters, submarines, and unmanned robots exploring the surface of Mars.

In all these situations, it is particularly important that as many potential causes of malfunction as possible be predicted beforehand so they can be avoided. Although one way to predict such failures is to test the system itself or physical models of it under a wide variety of circumstances, doing so can be very time consuming and expensive, and even very extensive testing can fail to uncover flaws that could lead to malfunction under circumstances that are difficult to predict but still likely to occur at some point in the system's lifetime.

One way to fill the void that results from the inability to perform exhaustive tests is to verify the correct operation of the system using techniques first derived for use in mathematical proofs. For example, certain kinds of computer software can be verified based on the software's source code without the need to run the software at all, much less in a very wide variety of circumstances. One benefit of this approach is that it does not rely on the ability of human engineers to predict all the conditions the software might face in the field. Instead, it concludes that the software will or will not behave correctly in *all* circumstances by drawing conclusions based on premises using rules of logic similar to those used in proving mathematical theorems.

Although these "formal methods" for verifying software become increasingly difficult to apply with complete certainty as the size of the software grows, their ability to provide a higher degree of reliability than experiment-based techniques can confer a significant benefit, particularly in cases, such as spacecraft, in which the system that requires verification is complex, capable of causing significant injury, and difficult or impossible to repair once in use. As it becomes possible to use computers to design and simulate the operation of increasingly complex physical products more accurately, it will become increasingly possible to use a combination of proof-based methods and computer simulation to test a wider and wider range of products using computers alone, thereby avoiding the need to build and test expensive physical prototypes and increasing the reliability and safety of the final products.

5

SIMULATION: CREATING WORLDS INSIDE A COMPUTER

A simulator is a machine or software that creates an illusion of the real world. For example, a *flight simulator* creates the illusion of being a pilot inside an airplane. Most people who are not pilots are familiar with flight simulators, which consist entirely of software that runs on a personal computer and displays three-dimensional animated images of the ground and sky as seen from within a cockpit and that allows the user to play the role of pilot using a mouse, keyboard, and possibly a joystick to control the movement of the "plane." Professional flight simulators, used to train pilots, may also include a physical cockpit in which the pilot-in-training sits while using the simulator. Such a cockpit may include controls, such as a yoke, and instruments, such as an altimeter and *barometer,* that mimic those found in real aircraft. The cockpit may even be capable of rotating and vibrating to simulate the physical forces a pilot would experience in a real cockpit. The cockpit may sit in front of a screen or be surrounded by screens on all sides that display realistic animated images to complete the illusion of piloting a real airplane.

Simulators provide many advantages over the real-world situations they are intended to imitate, such as:

- **Safety.** Simulators enable people to safely study and practice in environments that in the real world can be dangerous, even life threatening. Pilots can learn how to fly a plane in a storm at night, soldiers can learn how to engage in combat, and surgeons can learn how to perform surgery, all without any risk of physical harm to themselves or others. Those who graduate from such training are then less likely to cause harm in the real world.

- **Cost.** Although creating a simulator can be expensive, using a simulator to simulate an environment often is less expensive than studying or practicing in the real environment itself. Simulating the effects of a high-speed crash on an automobile frame is less expensive than building a prototype of such a frame just to destroy it for purposes of studying how it deforms under impact.

- **Control.** The conditions created by a simulator can be controlled very precisely, thereby making it possible to study or practice in certain conditions repeatedly, even if such conditions occur infrequently or are hard to replicate in the real world. A pilot can practice flying in a hurricane 10 times in one day, a surgeon can practice performing surgery to remove a rare kind of tumor, and local governments can simulate the response of their health care systems to influenza pandemics, all at the touch of a button. This ability to control conditions by a simulator can produce increased readiness to handle a real situation under those conditions effectively.

- **Flexibility.** Although simulators emulate the real world, they are not constrained by the limitations of the real world. As a result, simulators can create conditions that are not only unusual but even impossible in the real world. A flight simulator can test the ability of a pilot to fly a jet plane at 3,000 miles (4,828 km) an hour to improve the pilot's reflexes, although no real jet plane can fly that quickly. Automobile engineers can test the response of a car's brakes on surfaces with higher or lower friction than exist in the real world to better understand how to optimize the performance of the brakes under normal conditions. Just as science fiction that pushes past the boundaries of the possible has inspired scientists and engineers to consider new possibilities, so too do simulators that are not constrained by the laws of nature enable researchers and inventors to better understand and control real-world systems.

The rest of this chapter explores a wide range of situations that can now be simulated for use in government, education, health care, the military, scientific research, engineering, and entertainment.

SIMULATORS FOR TRAINING

The effectiveness of simulators at mimicking the real world makes them popular training tools for many occupations. Flight training simulators are used in the aviation industry and the military to train pilots and members of flight crews. These simulators are used for several types of training, including teaching pilots how to operate different aircraft systems, training flight crews in emergency procedures, and training aircraft maintenance workers in diagnosing

NASA research pilot Gordon Fullerton "flies" in the MD-11 flight simulator as part of the Propulsion Controlled Aircraft (PCA) project in 1998.   *(NASA Dryden Flight Research Center [NASA-DFRC])*

system failures. Flight simulator systems range from computer-based software simulators to cockpit replicas that provide both ultrarealistic visual displays and motion systems so the pilots in training can experience the physical movements they would encounter flying a real plane.

Many of today's high-end software flight simulators run on the Windows and Mac platforms with no additional hardware requirements. The most popular of these are the Microsoft Flight Simulator and Laminar Research's X-Plane. Although these simulators can be used in the home as entertainment, they are also used by professional pilots in private companies and the military as training aids.

Flight simulators that replicate the interior of an airplane cockpit are known as full flight simulators (FFS). The most sophisticated FFS systems are capable of movement with six degrees of freedom and provide realistic engine sounds and a feeling of force on the pilot controls. An FFS system is controlled by complex computer software that processes input from the control hardware and synchronizes the visual, motion, and sound feedback provided to the pilot. Such systems can realistically emulate the experience of flying a real airplane without the expense and risk of harm that comes with real flight. As a result, FFS systems can be used to train pilots to fly in hazardous conditions without exposing the trainees to any real danger and without damaging any real aircraft.

In the field of health care, simulators are used to train medical personnel in routine procedures, such as drawing blood, as well as in emergency procedures and more complicated surgical techniques. For example, at the Washington University School of Medicine, a computer-based endoscopic simulator is used to train medical students to guide an endoscopic tube through the interior of a patient's body.

Medical simulators often consist of computer programs that illustrate patient symptoms and provide tutorials on treatment alternatives. One such program is ACLS Interactive! This interactive computer-based tutorial provides realistic patient scenarios to help train paramedics for advanced cardiac life support certification. The program includes simulated tools such as oxygen, defibrillator, and endotracheal tubes that are used for treating emergency cardiac situations. There are also medical simulators that use special-purpose devices to make the simulation more realistic, such as a machine that simulates various sounds a patient's heart might make. The most sophisticated medical simulators use a mannequin, known as a patient simulator, to provide a realistic computer-

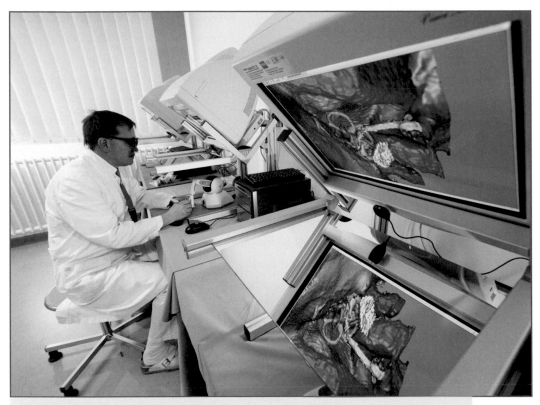

Dirk Esser performs virtual bone surgery on the middle ear using the Voxel-man simulator during a workshop in 2006.   *(AP Images)*

controlled model that presents symptoms, drives monitor systems, and responds to treatment, all in an attempt to provide the medical trainee with an environment that is as close to treating a live human patient as possible.

Military units use computer software to simulate combat conditions for training purposes. The most advanced combat simulators, such as Lockheed Martin's Combat Convoy System, immerse military personnel in virtual combat environments created with realistic 3-D modeling. The Combat Convoy System provides a full-scale model of a military vehicle with mounted weapons. Trainees are positioned in and around the vehicle and surrounded by screens that depict a landscape complete with roads, forests, mountains, and buildings. Realistic enemy troops are also depicted. Trainees come under attack by the enemy troops, and the experience is enhanced by audio and visual combat effects.

The military also makes use of simulators that are built into combat vehicles. These simulators allow soldiers to experience a realistic reproduction of a specific type of terrain, from jungle to desert to an urban environment with multiple civilians present. A combat vehicle simulator can be operated in a cargo plane as the vehicle is being transported to a combat area. The terrain simulator in one of these training vehicles requires a complex database of digitized information often derived from classified government materials.

Manufacturing is another industry that uses simulators for training purposes. Such simulators are usually computer-based systems that present users with an interactive model that simulates electrical and mechanical failures. Personnel learn how to troubleshoot failures and perform routine maintenance using the simulator. For example, training simulators are often used for chemical plants and for fossil fuel and nuclear power plants. A wide range of operations and malfunctions can be simulated without risk and at a much less expense compared to conducting training using actual power plant equipment.

Manufacturing simulations are also used for design and training with large-scale automated manufacturing operations, such as an automobile assembly line that uses robots. A software program, such as Honeywell's Shadow Plant, can be used to mimic the operations of an entire manufacturing plant to allow engineers to fine-tune manufacturing processes. It can also be used to train operators in procedures for starting up, running, and shutting down plant machinery.

SIMULATORS FOR ENTERTAINMENT

Many of today's most popular video games are a form of simulator. The player is presented with a realistic 3-D world where challenges are presented and a storyline emerges based on the player's actions. The 3-D world of the story may resemble the real world, or it may depict a completely fictional or fantasy world. The Halo series of videogames is perhaps the most famous example of this type of game. Also known as a "first-person shooter," Halo depicts the exploits of a genetically enhanced supersoldier as he tries to save mankind from destruction. The immense popularity of this type of game is based on the realism with which the simulated world is depicted. The player controls the interaction between combatants as they use their weaponry and react to natural elements such as fire and smoke, all of which interact realistically with each other. For example, shooting a barrel of oil causes the barrel to explode, and the force of the explosion causes other nearby objects to move or even ignite, as they would in the real world. Such effects are created by modeling the real-world laws of physics within the virtual world of the video game.

Another category of video game provides a simulated world in which no goals are explicitly laid out by the makers of the games. Instead, it is left up to the player to choose his or her own goals and to pursue them in the best way he or she sees fit. These games allow the player to assume the role of manager. In management simulation games, the player operates a sports team, a business, or some other type of institution. Examples of this type of game include the Madden NFL series, Theme Park World, and The Movies. The player has control over a variety of resources and manages them to produce various outcomes. The simulators in these games create the response of people in the game world—such as a team of football players, theme park visitors, or movie actors—to the actions taken by the game player. The success of such games relies on simulators that are complex enough to produce simulated behavior—such as the decision of people to flock to a new theme park ride when a hot dog stand is placed nearby—that is realistic but not so simple that it can be easily predicted by the game player. Unrealistic behavior will cause the game player to become frustrated, while overly predictable behavior will quickly lead to a boring game. Creating simulators that strike the right balance is one of the main challenges faced by those who design such games.

In city-building games, the player is an urban planner who designs a city and then creates a budget for its inhabitants. One of the best-known city-building games is SimCity, which has been upgraded and expanded through several versions over the years. In this game, the player can divide the city into commercial, industrial, and residential zones and then add buildings, design a power grid, create a transportation system, and raise taxes to pay for it all. The player must also react to the effects of natural disasters, such as tornadoes, fires, and earthquakes. In response to the player-manager's decisions and such natural events, the city's virtual inhabitants make their own decisions, such as whether to stay in the city and, if so, where to live, work, and play. Such simulated actions affect the city itself, such as by increasing tax revenues and attracting tourists to the city. Characteristics of the city, such as its crime rate, can usually be affected by multiple alternative actions, such as hiring more police officers and building more parks. Such choices make the game more challenging and enjoyable.

In life simulation games, the player manages a society or life form. This type of game is also referred to as a "god game," since the player has extensive control over the lives of communities or even individual characters. The most popular of the social simulation games is The Sims, in which a player controls social interactions between virtual characters living in an environment that resembles the suburban United States. The characters, their homes, and other aspects of their lives are created by the player, who then can control their moods and desires. The player then watches as the characters act out their lives, such as waking up and preparing for their day, going to work and school, and interacting with one another by talking, throwing parties, and going out on dates. The player can choose to intervene as much or as little as desired in the lives of the game's virtual inhabitants.

The game Spore allows player to create and manage artificial life forms. It consists of several distinct phases. In the early phases, a player begins by creating a microscopic organism. The game simulates the evolution of the microbe as it moves through several stages until the player is allowed to "edit" the creature and add arms, legs, and other appendages. After passing through several more phases, each of which increases the sociability and intelligence of the creature, a tribal phase is entered. Primitive communities of creatures can be formed at this point. The tribal phase is followed by a civilization phase, in which more complex societies are formed. Finally, a space phase involves interstellar exploration. Each phase of Spore is intended to simulate a different aspect of biological and cultural evolution. Players may stay at a phase for as long as they wish, which allows a great deal of flexibility in how the game is played. Although the game is intended primarily as entertainment, it can be used to provide students with a basic overview of real-world evolution through its use of simulated evolution.

Early simulation games ran on personal computers and game machines. With the growth of the Internet, large-scale games played by a large number of people became possible. These games are known as "massively multiplayer online games" (MMOG). It is common for many thousands of people to simultaneously play a single MMOG. This type of game may be played exclusively online, or it may be played on a game console that can access the Internet. Most of the newer game consoles support Internet access, including the Wii, Xbox 360, Nintendo DS, and PlayStation 3. A characteristic of MMOG simulation games is that they take place in a simulated world that is persistent, meaning that it continues even as individual players come and go. Examples of MMOG

`11001110100101010100110010111011010100101001`

Second Life

Second Life (SL) is a simulated three-dimensional world accessible online and was developed in 2003 by Linden Lab, an Internet company based in San Francisco, California. Since its introduction, Second Life has had a major impact on how simulation games are perceived and used on the Internet. The Second Life experience is focused on creativity and community. As a game, it has no specific objective or rules—there is no winning or losing. The popularity of Second Life is evidenced by the fact that in 2008, 15 million registered users were reported by Linden Lab.

There is no charge to register as SL player and interact in the SL world. After downloading a free client program called Second Life Viewer, players select avatars that will be their representations in the game. SL avatars are three-dimensional digital personas that can be created in almost any form, including human, animal, vegetable, or mineral. Players, known as Residents, communicate through their avatars using local chat, which is public, or the more private instant messaging.

An important part of SL is a 3-D modeling tool that allows Residents to build objects in the SL world using simple geometric shapes. With external software tools, Residents can also create more complex objects that have textures and animation. Its terms of service allow creators to retain full rights to their virtual creations.

Internally, SL makes use of a *physics engine* to simulate the interactions of objects in a simulated world. This software engine applies laws of Newtonian physics to simulate gravity, collisions, and momentum. The engine "grounds" avatars in the SL world, forcing them to move around and over objects rather than through them. The realism of SL's virtual world is made possible by the simulation calculated by the physics engine.

Residents of SL can partake in a wide variety of activities. Sports are available, including football, wrestling, boxing, and auto racing. Residents can be spectators or train to be participants. Gaming and role-playing areas are available. Residents can express themselves creatively through the visual and performing arts, then exhibit their artwork or participate in a performance. It also offers many opportunities for social interaction. Parties, nightclubs, workshops, shopping, and fashion shows are all available in the SL world.

(continues)

`11001110100101010100110010111011010100101001`

001101010010100111010110101010101011001010000 1

(continued)

There is an economy and an internal form of currency, the Linden dollar (L$). All types of virtual goods and services can be bought and sold with L$. The SL economy is fully integrated into its virtual world. Residents may buy Linden currency with U.S. dollars and then use the Linden dollars to buy and sell virtual goods and services. There is a real estate market that allows Residents to build homes, businesses, and communities. Linden Lab has stated that $35 million in U.S. dollars is traded among Residents each month.

The state of the SL economy is subject to the same marketplace pressures as is an economy in the real world. Many real-world companies have an SL presence, including American Apparel, Starwood Hotels, and Scion. There are people who make a full-time living from virtual businesses in SL.

Second Life is used as an educational tool by many schools and institutions. Several hundred universities throughout the world offer courses or conduct research in SL. There are also educational institutions that exist solely in SL. Another crossover from real life to the SL world is in the area of health care. Several hundred health care support groups in SL allow Residents to share information and get support for specific health issues and diseases, such as cancer and autism. The growth of education and health care groups in SL shows that it is an important tool for bringing people together and creating a sense of community.

001101010010100111010110101010101011001010000 1

simulation games include World of Warcraft, Motor City Online, and The Sims Online. In 2010, World of Warcraft was the leader in MMOG gaming market, with more than 11.5 million monthly subscribers.

Simulation games are sometimes used by educators as teaching aids. Teachers who are willing to invest the time to incorporate a simulation game into their curriculum are able to provide students with a realistic experience of concepts taught in the classroom but without the expense or potential danger of exposing the students directly to the phenomena being simulated. For example, a game that includes a realistic physics simulator can enable students to learn about the physics of fire without requiring the students to interact with real fires and without requiring the teacher to obtain the permits necessary to create fires in the classroom. Furthermore, because simulation games are intended to present the results of simulations in an entertaining way, such games can engage students and keep them interested in a subject in a way that may not be possible with more conventional teaching techniques. For example, SimCity has been used in classrooms to help educate students about urban planning in a way that may hold the interest of students more strongly than a set of equations that relates tax policies to population growth.

SIMULATORS FOR SCIENTIFIC EXPERIMENTATION

Simulations of chemistry and biology laboratories have been created by research scientists and educators to support virtual experimentation. Scientists can perform virtual experiments more quickly and more safely and at a lower cost than experiments in the real world. For example, pharmaceutical companies can use virtual experiments to test the effects of drugs on the human body. Simulators are also used to aid in automatic drug discovery, which is accomplished by screening a large number of chemicals and testing their effectiveness against a target disease or condition.

In the academic arena, virtual labs allow students to interact with a wide variety of materials and properties in a controlled environment. An example of an educational virtual lab has been developed by the ChemCollective group at Carnegie-Mellon University. Available online, the ChemCollective Web site provides a variety of student activities and experiments to conduct in the lab.

SIMULATORS IN THE SOCIAL SCIENCES

Computer simulation in the social sciences often focuses on the study of adaptive behaviors that emerge in social systems. This type of simulation often uses "agent-based" simulation. A computer-simulated society is created, and an individual entity, the agent, is placed in the simulated society. The behavior of this agent is then observed. An example of the use of this type of simulation is the study of dating patterns, such as how many people an individual will date before deciding on "the right one." One of the criticisms of these simulations is that they are usually based on simplified mathematical models that do not reflect the complexity of actual human society.

Another type of social simulation is concerned with the growth of social systems. One of the most famous examples of this type of simulator is the Game of Life. This simulation was created by Cambridge University mathematician John Conway in 1970. The Game of Life consists of a simple graphical grid that contains a collection of cells that use a handful of mathematical rules to live, multiply, and die. The game requires no intervention by a human player except for the initial placement of cells on the grid. Once this initial choice is made, the game plays by itself automatically. The resulting changes in the simulated population of cells are typically displayed onscreen as an animated display of the population's changing state. Many free versions of the Game of Life are available for play on the Internet. Conway devised the game in response to a challenge by the renowned mathematician John von Neumann to create a virtual machine, or automaton, that could create copies of itself.

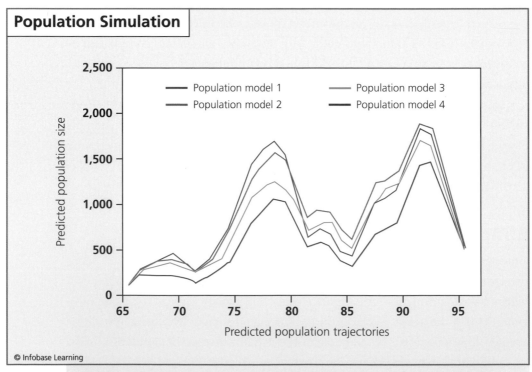

Population Simulation

© Infobase Learning

Computer software can be used to predict variations in the size of a population over time in response to factors including available food, climate, reproduction rate, disease, and natural disasters. Different mathematical models of population change (such as those represented by the four colored plots in the accompanying graph) can lead to different predictions by the computer.

The Game of Life is not intended to simulate changes in populations in the real world. Simulators for modeling population growth, however, do exist. Such simulators can mimic how a population of humans or other living organisms grows and shrinks over time in response to factors such as birth rate, life expectancy, migration rate, incidence of disease, availability of food, and natural disasters. As a result, government agencies can use such simulations in efforts to plan for changes in population that might otherwise be difficult to predict based merely on past and current trends. Furthermore, various population simulators are provided online for educational and informational purposes, such as the one at www.breathingearth.net, which provides an animated map of the world that illustrates births, deaths, and CO_2 emissions in various countries over time.

SIMULATORS FOR ENGINEERING

In most engineering disciplines, the use of computer simulators has become a standard part of the design process. Since engineering designs usually involve problem solving and experimentation, a simulator can be used to test the results

(continues on page 78)

NASA engineers used software to simulate the operation of the Mars Exploration Rover *Spirit.*   *(NASA Jet Propulsion Laboratory [NASA-JPL])*

Jay Forrester, Creator of Some of the Earliest Computer Simulators

Jay Forrester was born in 1918 on a ranch near Anselmo, Nebraska. The ranch had no electrical power, so while in high school, Forrester built a 12-volt wind-driven electrical system of old car parts to give the ranch electricity for the first time. Although he had a scholarship to study agriculture, he instead chose to enroll in the engineering college at the University of Nebraska in 1936. Upon graduation in 1939 with a bachelor's degree in electrical engineering, Forrester took up a research position at MIT and earned a master's degree in electrical engineering in 1945. He remained at MIT for the rest of his career.

Pat Youtz, Stephen Dodd, and Jay Forrester (pictured left to right) examine a finished electrostatic storage tube for Project Whirlwind in 1950. Forrester was also the designer of some of the earliest computer simulators. *(MITRE Corporate Archives)*

10011101001010101001100101110110101001010 01

His earliest work at MIT reflected the military demands of the time. Forrester worked on developing servomechanisms to control radar antennas and gun mounts and in 1942 was dispatched to Pearl Harbor to repair problems on the experimental units that were installed on the USS *Lexington*. The ship left the harbor with Forrester still onboard hard at work and soon encountered heavy Japanese fire; Forrester later recalled this as a "concentrated immersion in how research and theory are related to practical end uses." In 1944, he became involved with a project building an aircraft flight simulator, which developed into the Whirlwind I computer, the first computer that operated in real time and used video displays. As the director of the MIT Digital Computer Laboratory from 1946 to 1951, Forrester was responsible for the design and construction of the Whirlwind I system. While working on the project, Forrester developed magnetic core memory, which was the predecessor of modern random access memory (RAM). The Whirlwind became the basis for the Semi-Automatic Ground Environment (SAGE) air defense system after the Navy took a serious interest in defensive improvements following the onset of the cold war and the nuclear advancements of the Soviet Union. The Whirlwind, as the most advanced computer available to the military, was selected, and in 1953, Forrester's improved magnetic core memory was added to it. SAGE began operating in 1958 and continued to be used until the 1980s as the nation's air defense system.

Forrester continued research in electrical and computer engineering until 1956, when he concluded that the heyday of engineering pioneers was over and left engineering to go into management to take on newer challenges. He joined the faculty at the MIT Sloan School of Management, where he later became the Germeshausen Professor Emeritus of Management. Early in his time at Sloan, Forrester interviewed a group of executives from General Electric (GE) who came to MIT for help with running a GE appliance plant. The plant went through periods of peak demand followed by deep slumps that were severe enough to force layoffs. The executives wanted to know what, if anything, could be done to run the plant in a more consistent manner. After the interview, Forrester plotted the impacts of hiring and inventory decisions made by GE; the resulting chart looked very similar to the technical patterns he previously observed in servo-driven cannons, in which the first shot would overshoot the mark and the next would miss

(continues)

10011101001010101001100101110110101001010 01

001101010010100111010110101010101011001010000 1

(continued)

the mark in the other direction trying to overcompensate. It took several cycles to hit the target. One of Forrester's graduate students wrote a computer program to better handle the analysis. Forrester called this method of analysis "system dynamics," which can be used for extensive study of competition, innovation strategies, and firm behavior. It can also be used to model environmental, political, and economic behaviors. It is particularly well suited to modeling and predicting changes that occur over time and their effects on equilibrium. Forrester believed that most social organizations are substantially more complex than most people can understand unaided by technology, and, thus, unexpected and unintended behavior is likely to take place if decisions are made based on individual managers' theories of how the world should work. Instead, using system dynamics to analyze an issue removes the erroneous human element and suggests a more accurate, albeit possibly counterintuitive, solution to the situation. A system dynamics problem is solved using a computer simulator that behaves based on available information that has been entered into the model and is able to isolate and independently operate the complex variables of the system. The model makes it possible to observe the described system and its behavioral effects and evaluate whether such effects and system traits are desirable or intended. One of the consistent findings of system dynamics analysis was that it was not the competition but the firm's internal policies that were responsible for its troubles over time. It is possible

001101010010100111010110101010101011001010000 1

(continued from page 75)
of different design variables. For example, an engineer who is designing an aircraft wing can use a software simulator to study the flow of air around the wing, trying out different shapes with a simulator before deciding on the optimal design.

Computer-aided engineering (CAE) uses software to simulate, analyze, design, and manufacture mechanical devices. CAE systems are based on 3-D graphical representations of design objects. Simulation results are also represented graphically. For example, small arrows may show the direction of force or wind, and color may be used to represent heat. CAE simulators are widely used in the automotive industry to evaluate potential stresses on the body of an automobile, including heat, friction, and collisions. CAE is also used by aeronautical

to identify these points of internal resistance and use them as leverage points for intervention.

The first articles on system dynamics appeared in the *Harvard Business Review* in 1958, followed by Forrester's book entitled *Industrial Dynamics*, published in 1961. In this book, he relied on system dynamics to analyze industrial business development. Forrester's subsequent work, *Urban Dynamics*, published in 1969, suggested that broader social problems not limited to business organizations could also be modeled and studied with system dynamics. This idea attracted much attention. This was followed by another work, *World Dynamics*, which discussed modeling the relationship between world capital flows, population, natural resources, food production, and other issues concerning global sustainability. *The Limits to Growth*, a book produced by Forrester's team at MIT, modeled a grim future for the planet as the natural resources run out and actions that negatively impact the environment continued, but it also suggested that sustained and comfortable existence is possible if humanity accepts a future with less economic growth in return. The book was highly criticized for being overly negative and neglecting accepted economic theories. Nevertheless, it also became a rallying point for the global environmental movement.

Forrester received the IEEE Computer Pioneer Award in 1982 and the National Medal of Technology in 1989. He was inducted into the Operational Research Hall of Fame in 2006.

engineers and by mechanical engineers who work on many types of consumer products, from cameras to vacuum cleaners.

Civil and structural engineers use simulators to test new materials for construction. They also use them to ensure the safety of structures and to find cost-effective and environmentally sound solutions for design problems. For example, following Hurricane Katrina, the mechanical engineering firm Mechanical Solutions, Inc. (MSI), used simulation to evaluate the design of a pumping station in New Orleans. Simulation software evaluated the effects of vibrations from machinery on the stability of the pumping station platform.

Electrical engineers who design computer circuits also use simulation software to analyze design variables. One of the most popular of these simulators is

SPICE (Simulation Program with Integrated Circuit Emphasis), which was first developed by the University of California at Berkeley in the 1970s. The most current version, SPICE3, has been available at no charge online since 2000. SPICE is considered a fundamental tool for electrical engineers because it allows them to simulate how the circuits they design will operate in the real world without the need to build and test the circuits themselves.

Engineering in the world today is computer and simulator intensive. With simulation, designs for new machines and other types of systems can be tested and modified before they are ever built. This process helps build better systems, lowers engineering costs, and allows engineers to be more productive.

CONCLUSIONS

Although simulators of various kinds have existed since before computers were created, it is only within the last decade that personal computers became powerful enough to run simulators that convincingly imitate the sights and sounds of the real world. For example, for most of the history of computers, hardware for generating three-dimensional animated graphics was first funded and developed by the military, after which it trickled down into less-expensive graphics accelerator cards that could be used inside personal computers to power video games and scientific applications. In recent years, however, the development path has flipped. Private companies first develop high-end graphics accelerator cards for use in video games, and such cards are then purchased by the military for combat simulations. The same is true for much of the physics-simulating software that can display realistic animations of fire, flowing water, and objects with moving parts flying through space and bouncing off one another. The result is that the average computer user now has immediate access to each new generation of powerful simulators at essentially the same time as do governments and universities. Although most home users employ such simulators purely for entertainment, they can just as readily be used for scientific experimentation, engineering, and education.

A simulator for a video game need only be capable of showing a tire bouncing down a hill in a way that *appears* accurate to the casual viewer. For a simulator to be useful for scientists and engineers, however, it must be capable of simulating the tire's behavior in a way that *is* accurate, in the sense that the simulated behavior very closely matches the behavior a tire would exhibit under the same conditions in the real world. Simulators are becoming increasingly accurate in this sense for simulating phenomena such as the movement of solid objects and the operation of electrical circuits, which are well understood by physicists. In such contexts, simulators can be used to predict how physical systems will behave under real-world conditions and thereby potentially make new scientific discoveries without the need to perform experiments in the real world.

Many simulators become more accurate when run on more powerful computer hardware. Weather forecasting software that runs on a particular computer, for example, might need to treat every 10-square-foot (3.6 m²) of surface of the Earth as a single unit of space, thereby ignoring differences in temperature and other conditions within that space, in order to produce a prediction quickly enough to be useful. If the same software is run on more powerful computer hardware, it might be able to treat every one-square foot of surface as a single unit of space, thereby enabling more accurate weather predictions to be generated. For this reason, we should expect simulators in many fields to produce improved results as computer hardware continues to grow exponentially more powerful, even if the simulator algorithms themselves do not improve.

This trend holds promise for increasing the usefulness of simulators to emulate highly complex natural phenomena, such as the motion of fluids and gases, and social phenomena, such as public behavior in response to an outbreak of influenza or a terrorist attack. Such phenomena are governed by such a large number of subtle and interacting parameters that they cannot be simulated accurately by computers in the absence of very powerful computer hardware that starts from large quantities of detailed data. For example, accurately simulating the movement of pollutants in a water supply can require simulating each individual molecule to produce an accurate result. It is now becoming possible to simulate such movement using either state-of-the-art supercomputers or large networks of less-powerful computers working together within a few hours rather than a few years. Furthermore, as scientists' understanding of physics improves, they can use such knowledge to improve simulation algorithms so that they run more quickly and accurately, even on the same hardware. This combination of improved hardware and improved simulation software for running on that hardware is in the process of ushering in a new era of using simulators to explore the natural world in ways never before possible.

6

WEATHER: MAPPING THE PAST, PREDICTING THE FUTURE

Humanity has shown an interest in weather forecasting since the earliest days of civilization. Around 650 B.C.E., the Babylonians used the appearance of clouds and other optical phenomena in the sky, such as coronas and halos, to predict changes in the weather. In 300 B.C.E., the Chinese created an annual calendar based on their knowledge of astronomy. This calendar divided the year into 24 festivals, with each festival associated with a distinct weather pattern.

Around 340 B.C.E., the Greek philosopher Aristotle wrote a treatise called *Meteorologica*. The modern name for the study of weather, meteorology, takes its name from this work. This treatise discussed many of Aristotle's theories about Earth science and covered such weather topics as wind, clouds, rain, lightning, thunder, and rainbows. For nearly 2,000 years, Aristotle's theories about weather predominated among scientists and intellectuals. It was not until the 17th century that some of his theories were disproved.

Across the centuries, most cultures have observed weather patterns and taken notice of the association between one weather event and another. Being able to predict weather has always been important for farmers, sailors, and those whose livelihoods depend on weather conditions. Many societies have a body of folklore and traditions related to weather predictions. For example, it might be believed that if the sunset is very red, the following day will bring good weather. One of our modern traditions, Groundhog Day, possibly has its roots in an ancient Celtic belief that a sunny day at winter's midpoint meant that winter would be long and cold.

These traditions make weather predictions by observing weather patterns and attempting to extrapolate the observed patterns into the future. For example, if heavy snow is observed in the month of February for 10 years in a row, traditional weather prediction techniques may draw the conclusion that it will always be snowy in February. Such inferences, however, are not always reliable; it is always possible that there will be no snow in a particular February. Simple extrapolation of past patterns into the future will fail to predict such events, which do not fit the previously observed pattern.

The ability of early weather forecasters to predict weather accurately was also significantly restricted by limitations on communication. For example, when bad weather was being experienced in one area, there was no quick and reliable way to let other communities know that bad weather was coming their way. Furthermore, inability to share weather information across geographic regions made it difficult for weather forecasters to take into account regional and global events that are essential to predicting local weather accurately.

For farmers, a book called an almanac became a trusted source of weather information. An almanac contains an annual calendar along with information about cycles of the Moon, tides, and other astronomical occurrences for the year. The origins of the almanac date back to ancient times. Early almanacs often contained horoscopes and made predictions based on astrological principles. The first printed almanac was produced by Gutenberg in 1457, eight years before the famous Gutenberg bible. Perhaps the most famous almanac was published by Benjamin Franklin each year from 1732 to 1758. Franklin wrote his *Poor Richard's Almanac* under the pen name Richard Saunders and, in addition to weather information, included witty sayings and proverbs.

Almanacs are often associated with the idea of forecasting the weather far in advance, but only in modern times have almanacs included information about weather predictions. Two popular almanacs from the 18th and 19th centuries that are still in publication today include predictions about weather. The *Old Farmer's Almanac*, first published in 1792, and *The Farmers' Almanac*, which first appeared in 1818, each use a secret formula for predicting weather far in advance. These formulas are based on study of prevailing weather patterns, historical weather conditions, and solar activity to forecast the weather up to 18 months in advance.

Since technological advances now provide the writers of these almanacs with a large body of data about trends in weather patterns, both publications are able to claim a weather prediction success rate of at least 80 percent. This was not the case with almanacs published before the 20th century.

EARLY WEATHER PREDICTION MACHINES

Toward the end of the Renaissance, an increased desire began to arise for a more scientific understanding of weather conditions and more accuracy in predicting them. Measuring instruments were being developed for many scientific disciplines, including astronomy, surveying, and navigation. In the area of weather, instruments were needed to measure temperature, moisture, pressure, and other atmospheric properties.

The *hygrometer,* an instrument that measures the moisture content in air, was first developed by the German cardinal and philosopher Nicholas of Cusa in 1450. At about the same time, the Italian priest and philosopher Leon Battista Alberti invented the *anemometer,* a device used to measure wind speed. In the 16th century, the renowned Italian scientist Galileo Galilei and several other scientists working separately developed the thermometer and a related instrument, the thermoscope, for measuring air temperature. In 1643, the Italian physicist and mathematician Evangelista Torricelli is believed to have invented the barometer, an instrument that measures atmospheric pressure.

The development of these instruments led to the establishment of weather station facilities. These facilities were equipped for weather observation using thermometers, barometers, hygrometers, anemometers, and rain gauges. In 1654, the first weather observation network was established by Ferdinando II de' Medici. Weather conditions were documented and collected from weather stations in Florence, Milan, Paris, Warsaw, and other locations.

The next technological leap in the study of weather was brought on by the invention of the electromagnetic telegraph by Baron Shilling in 1832. The telegraph made it possible to quickly collate weather information from many different locations. Data about atmospheric conditions could then be used to create weather maps and to attempt to forecast the weather based on information available in the maps.

The development of instruments to aid in weather observation and the establishment of weather stations that gathered and classified weather data added significantly to the body of scientific knowledge about weather. The invention of the telegraph allowed scientists eventually to gather worldwide weather data, chart global weather systems, and predict future weather trends. These events mark the birth of synoptic weather forecasting, whereby a prior weather pattern is used as a guide to forecast future weather events.

Admiral Fitzroy's barometer was consulted by crews before their voyages at many ports in the 18th century. Barometers, which measure atmospheric pressure, are still important tools for weather prediction.   *(Chris Pearsall/Alamy)*

0011010100101001110101101010101011001010000 1

Why Predicting the Weather Is So Difficult: The "Butterfly Effect"

Astronomers can predict the precise locations of the moons of Jupiter 10 years into the future. Physics simulators can predict the exact zigzagging paths that pool balls will take on a pool table when struck at any speed and angle. Pollsters can even predict with great accuracy which candidate for political office will win an election based on initial exit poll results from a small percentage of voters. Even so, weather forecasters still cannot predict tomorrow's weather without a wide margin of error and cannot predict the weather two weeks from now at all. Why?

The answer is that weather systems and other *complex systems* such as stock markets exhibit a characteristic known as "sensitive dependence on initial conditions." This means that even a tiny change in environmental conditions today can lead to significant and unpredictable changes in weather tomorrow. In the context of weather, this phenomenon has come to be known as the *"butterfly effect,"* based on the idea that a butterfly flapping its wings in Brazil can create a typhoon in Japan. Edward Lorenz popularized this idea after he entered the number .506 into a computer weather simulation, instead of the more complete number .506127, because he assumed that the approximate number .506 would produce similar results. However, he found that even the tiny difference (.000127) between the number he entered and the "correct" number caused his weather simulator to produce an entirely different outcome. Lorenz developed a series of equations that describe a system that has come to be known as the Lorenz Attractor. The attractor, which is an example of a "chaotic" system because it exhibits a complex, nonrepeating pattern, has found applications in predicting changes in weather and climate over time.

In reality, the flap of a butterfly's wings might not affect the weather. Instead, the import of Lorenz's colorful idea for weather prediction is that failure to measure all characteristics of the environment today—such as temperature, pressure, and humidity—with extremely high accuracy will cause any predictions of tomorrow's weather based on those measurements be more inaccurate than one might expect and for such inaccuracies to grow significantly as predictions are made further and further into the future. This inability to predict the weather accurately results not only from our failure to completely understand how weather systems

0011010100101001110101101010101011001010000 1

10011101001010101001100101110110101001010011

Lorenz Attractor

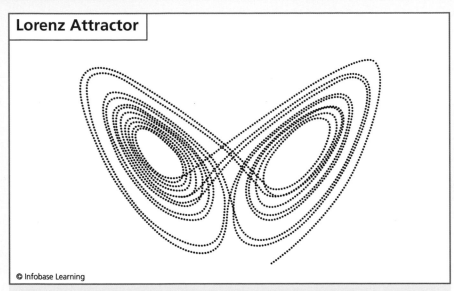

© Infobase Learning

The Lorenz Attractor, named after the mathematician Edward Lorenz, is a nonrepeating pattern governed by a set of equations that exhibits chaotic properties. Lorenz is also responsible for coining the term *butterfly effect.* Perhaps coincidentally, the Lorenz Attractor both exhibits the butterfly effect and appears similar to a butterfly.

work but also from the nature of weather as a system that has sensitive dependence on initial conditions. As a result, even if we could develop a perfect understanding of the processes by which weather develops, we would still be limited in our ability to predict the weather if we could not measure today's weather conditions with extremely high accuracy and feed those measurements into weather models.

The butterfly effect is often misunderstood to imply that all attempts to make predictions about the future are futile. Not all systems exhibit the butterfly effect because not all systems exhibit sensitive dependence on initial conditions. Many natural and artificial systems, such as the motion of the stars and planets, the trajectory of a missile when fired from a missile launcher, and even the travel patterns of people on holidays follow predictable rules that are not sensitively dependent on initial conditions. As a result, the behavior of such systems can be predicted

(continues)

10011101001010101001100101110110101001010011

(continued)

with relatively high accuracy even if the initial measurements used to make those predictions are not entirely accurate. For example, the number of people who will travel by car on a particular highway on Labor Day can be predicted with high accuracy based on the numbers of people who traveled on that same highway on previous Labor Days, even if travel records from earlier years contain errors of a size that would cause a weather simulator to produce completely useless results. One ongoing challenge for scientists and engineers is to identify those systems, such as weather, that do exhibit the butterfly effect and those that do not so that the right prediction techniques can be applied in each case and so that any predictions made about systems that do follow the butterfly effect can be taken with a large grain of salt before being relied upon.

THE ROLE OF COMPUTER MODELS IN WEATHER PREDICTION

Many of the scientists who studied weather and developed instruments to measure atmospheric conditions from the 15th through the 19th centuries were mathematicians who developed equations to describe many of the physical aspects of the atmosphere. The next logical step was to use mathematical equations to forecast the weather. The Norwegian mathematician and physicist Vilhelm Bjerknes is considered by many to be the founder of modern weather forecasting. In 1904, Bjerknes published a paper that proposed using mathematical formulas and information about the current state of the atmosphere to predict future weather conditions. There was one major drawback to Bjerknes's proposal: There was no feasible way to complete the number of mathematical computations he proposed in a reasonable amount of time.

Bjerknes was not discouraged by his findings. He viewed forecasting as the main goal of weather research and trusted that future inventions would allow the required computations to be completed quickly enough to be useful in weather forecasting. In 1910, the British mathematician Lewis Fry Richardson further developed Bjerknes's proposal by spending several months solving, by hand, the differential equations needed to support weather prediction for a six-hour period into the future. Unfortunately, Richardson's prediction was highly inaccurate due to his failure to perform mathematical smoothing techniques on his data.

Despite the inaccuracy of his weather forecast, Richardson published in 1922 *Weather Prediction by Numerical Process.* In this book, he reported his results and then proposed a way to perform the calculations in a timely manner. Richardson's scheme required a roomful of people who would work out the large number of equations required for weather prediction and communicate the results of each stage of computation to one another. A very large room would be needed to hold the 64,000 people Richardson estimated would be required to perform the computations!

In 1943, a computing machine capable of doing the work that Richardson envisioned for a roomful of people became available. This machine was the ENIAC (Electronic Numerical Integrator and Calculator), the first automatic computer. John von Neumann, an eminent mathematician who was part of the team that developed the ENIAC, decided that one of the best tests of the new computer would be to apply it to the problem of *weather modeling.* A team of meteorologists and mathematicians was assembled at the Institute for Advanced Studies in Princeton, New Jersey. It took several years to refine the process proposed by Bjerknes and Richardson and to program the computer to execute it. Finally, in 1950, an accurate 24-hour forecast could be completed within 24 hours.

Weather predictions that are solved numerically by computer are often referred to as computer weather simulations or computer models. These simulations work by taking data from current weather conditions and applying the laws of physics and fluid dynamics to predict future atmospheric conditions. The fluids in this case are wind and water, and the data consist of measurements related to temperature, humidity, and atmospheric pressure.

Computer models have become important tools for meteorologists who predict the weather. They can help provide detailed weather forecasts for up to seven days in advance. For predictions that are weeks and months into the future, computer models can help meteorologists provide general outlooks about the possibility of certain weather conditions.

LONG-TERM CLIMATE MODELS

A climate model is another type of computer simulation that uses mathematical equations. A distinction needs to be made here between the terms *climate* and *weather.* Climate is the average weather over extended lengths of time, with day-to-day variations smoothed out. Weather is affected by all the variables of the atmosphere, which is what makes it difficult to predict more than a few days in advance. Climate, on the other hand, is determined by major forces that govern the energy balance of Earth. Energy is delivered to Earth in the form of solar heat. What happens to that heat when it reaches Earth is what creates the climate for various regions.

Climate models are most often used to study how Earth's climate would respond to increases in the amount of solar heat being absorbed by Earth's atmosphere as well as the impact of humanmade greenhouse gases on Earth's ability to cool itself. In order for Earth's climate to remain in balance, the flow of solar heat into the atmosphere must be offset by infrared energy moving out of the system.

A climate model uses equations to determine how Earth's atmosphere, land surfaces, oceans, and ice will respond to variances in solar heat. The effects of solar heat on both the surface of Earth and Earth's atmosphere are taken into account. The National Center for Atmospheric Research (NCAR) supports the development of several climate models, providing simulations of Earth's past, present, and future climates.

NCAR's climate models of the past are sophisticated numerical software packages designed to run on large supercomputers. They trace the climate time-line over hundreds or thousands of years using equations created from the laws of physics and chemistry. These equations are applied to data gathered from the evidence of climate changes that can be found above and below the surface of Earth. Paleoclimate models simulate the climate from millions of years in the past and help provide evidence about the sources of mass extinctions that occurred at different points in prehistory.

Climate models of the past give scientists insight into historical climate change and provide benchmarks for comparison with results from models of future climate. At NCAR, climate models that simulate Earth's future climate are focused on the problem of global warming. Climate simulations have already shown that the small increase in solar energy being delivered to Earth does not account for all the global warming of the past century. The majority

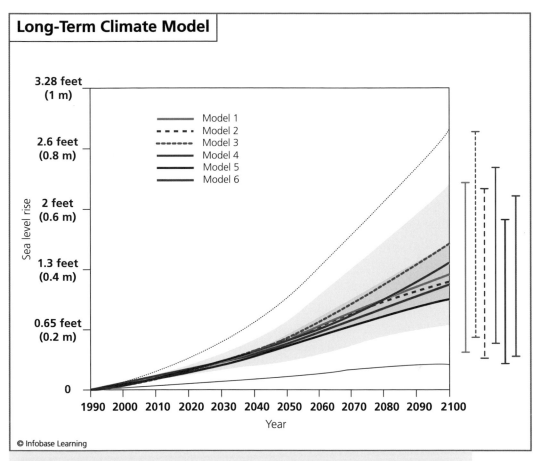

Long-Term Climate Model

Climate scientists use long-term climate models to predict probable future scenarios for global and regional climates. The figure shows an example in which six different climate models make six different predictions about sea level rise in the future. Although it is difficult to produce long-term climate models that are highly accurate, strong similarities among multiple climate models can provide indications that certain scenarios are significantly more likely to occur than others.

of the global warming is attributed to greenhouse gases emitted when fossil fuels are burned.

Climate models are created using data about the current and past states of atmospheric systems. The models are only as accurate as the data that are used. Another area for potential problems in climate modeling is in the area of calculation. Like all software, climate model programs are subject to programming errors that cause incorrect results to be reported.

Another challenge facing climate models is in the area of regional climate models. Trying to predict how various regions will respond to global climate changes is almost as difficult as making long-term weather predictions. Many variables come into play that create the need to use probabilities to make predictions about future regional climate changes.

SENSORS AND WEATHER PREDICTION

Besides requiring a valid set of equations, a computer weather model depends on accurate data. The basic instruments that were devised centuries ago to measure weather conditions are still used today to serve as weather sensors. Advances in technology have continued to improve in how weather data from sensors are gathered. One of the most important advances is in the use of weather balloons. The first meteorological weather balloons appeared in France in 1892. They were used to send thermometers, barometers, and hygrometers high into the atmosphere to measure temperature, pressure, and humidity.

Meteorologists faced challenges in retrieving data from these early balloons since they often drifted with the wind or burst at high altitudes. In the 1930s, the Finnish inventor Vilho Vaisala devised the radiosonde, a small radio transmitter that allows scientists to gather data from a balloon while it stays aloft. Since then, additional developments in the composition of the skin of weather balloons has led to zero-pressure and Mylar balloons that can be used at very high altitudes and remain aloft for months at a time. Weather balloons are now one of the most important means of gathering sensor information for weather forecasts. Each day, several hundred weather balloons are launched from locations around the world.

The weather satellite is another technological advance that has contributed greatly to improvements in the accuracy of weather forecasting. In 1960, the first polar-orbiting satellite was successfully launched for the purpose of mapping Earth's cloud cover from high altitudes. Since then, additional advances in sensor technology allow satellites to transmit data about atmospheric pressure and humidity as well as visual images.

Weather radar is an additional modern tool that aids in weather forecasting. This type of radar can locate precipitation, calculate its motion, and determine its type (i.e., rain, snow, sleet, or hail). The potential for weather

Weather balloons are used to carry instruments such as thermometers, barometers, and hygrometers, into the atmosphere for gathering weather data. Such instruments then transmit their readings back to meteorologists on the ground using radio signals.   *(AP Images)*

radar was first observed in World War II, when radar operators noticed that precipitation was picked up as a radar echo. In the years following the war, weather radar systems were widely developed and put into use in weather stations around the world.

UNDERSTANDING WEATHER PREDICTION ACCURACY

Despite exponential increases in computing power and the availability of increasingly large amounts of weather data from advanced tools such as satellites and radar, the accuracy of weather forecasts for periods of more than a few days has not increased proportionally. Due to the large number of atmospheric factors that affect weather, accurate predictions of weather beyond a few days are now seen as nearly impossible. Scientists have found that small differences in initial conditions can have large effects on the results of computations performed by computer weather simulators.

Today's meteorologists have come to understand that it is not possible to make detailed weather predictions for more than six to seven days in the future. In order to provide forecasts farther into the future, scientists give generalized outlooks rather than detailed predictions. These long-range outlooks differ from daily forecasts by not being specific about weather changes. Instead, they express the outlook in terms of averages, stating whether the average temperature and chances of rain or snow will be above or below normal. A weather forecaster will never predict that the high temperature a month in the future will be 72 degrees, because it is not possible using current technology to make such an accurate prediction.

Outlooks do not attempt to state that the weather will be cold or hot, wet or dry. They focus instead on shifts in the odds for change. For example, a weather forecaster may state that the chances of "warmer than average temperatures are 60 percent." This means that the chances of average temperatures are 33 percent, while the chances of colder temperatures are 7 percent. This type of long-range outlook is usually more accurate for temperature than it is for precipitation. When outlooks for precipitation are given, they are usually expressed in terms of the amount of precipitation only and do not try to predict whether it will be rain or snow.

The following are two different methods that are used to make short- and long-term predictions.

- Predictions for up to two weeks in the future are based on data about weather conditions throughout the world. These data are used as the initial setting in a computer weather model program, which applies the laws of physics to make a short-term prediction.
- Longer-term predictions, including months and years into the future, start with statistical information about current weather conditions and then factor in global information, such as ocean temperatures. Meteorologists are finding that ocean patterns that affect a large area, such as El Niño, play an important role in long-term weather forecasting.

Francis Beaufort, Creator of the "Beaufort Scale" for Measuring Wind Speed

Born in 1774 in County Meath, Ireland, Sir Francis Beaufort was an admiral of the British Royal Navy as well as a hydrographer who was responsible for the creation of the *Beaufort scale* that indicates wind force. He began his nautical career at 13 as a cabin boy in the Royal Navy. Beaufort soon began keeping a meteorological journal with brief comments on the weather, which he found useful and continued to do until his death.

Beaufort became a lieutenant at 22 and was assigned to command his first vessel, HMS *Woolwich,* on a hydrographic survey of the Rio de la Plata region in South America. While on this assignment, he began working on the wind force scale and weather notation coding, which he used to keep his meteorological journals. Beaufort was injured in 1812 while on another hydrographic assignment when he led the rescue of crewmembers who came

The British Admiral and hydrographer Francis Beaufort created a scale to measure the speed of wind at sea and on land referred to as the Beaufort scale. *(© National Maritime Museum, Greenwich, London)*

under hostile fire from pirates. A groin injury and a fractured hip caused him to spend several months recovering aboard the ship, and later that year, he was ordered to return home to fully recover. Beaufort never returned to active duty, although he remained in the navy until age 81.

In 1829, Beaufort became the Hydrographer to the Admiralty, a post that gave him responsibility for plotting hydrographic studies for British expeditions.

(continues)

(continued)

Four years later, the Beaufort weather notation was officially implemented as the notation used in log entries of the Royal Navy, and nine years later, in 1838, Beaufort's wind force scale was adopted by the navy as well. Beaufort was promoted to rear admiral in 1846 and received the title Knight Commander of the Order of the Bath in 1848. He retired from the navy in 1855 after 68 years of service.

Beaufort is remembered chiefly for his weather notation and wind force scale, now known as the Beaufort scale. However, the scale as we know it today is not the same as Beaufort's original because it underwent some major changes over the last 100 years. The original scale listed 13 degrees of wind strength, ranging from calm to hurricane. The degree was based on the amount of canvas carried by a fully rigged frigate ship, the prime ship of the British fleet in Beaufort's time.

The 1831 version of the wind scale described the first five degrees, or forces 0 to 4, as the ship with all sails clean and full in smooth water. The next forces, 5 to 9, described the ship's mission, chase, and its sail-carrying ability. Finally, forces 10 to 12 concerned the ship's ability to survive a storm or a hurricane. For example, at 0, the ship would be under all sails, while a ship under a whole gale, a force-10 wind, "could scarcely bear close-reefed main-topsail and reefed fore-sail," while a force-12 hurricane could not be withstood by any canvas. The scale was adopted because it had no ambiguities in its day, and any naval officer could accurately identify the force grade based on it. However, when the frigate ceased to be the prime ship of the navy, changes to the scale needed to take place to make it adaptable to the new conditions.

The new Beaufort scale referred to "states of the sea or degrees of motion of trees" instead of frigate's sails. However, these indicators were more ambiguous,

CONCLUSIONS

The remaining inaccuracies in today's weather forecasts can obscure the major advances that have been made in weather prediction. Everyone has had the experience of watching a weather forecast on television that predicts a sunny day while simultaneously watching heavy rain falling outside the window. Weather forecasts more than a day or two in advance are made with low confidence and remain subject to change at any time. State-of-the-art weather forecasting tech-

and additional refinements were needed. In 1946, the International Meteorological Committee extended the scale to 17 force values, with the added values to provide additional detail for hurricane winds. The ranges were now defined by the wind speed measured at a height of 10 meters above the surface, eliminating any inconsistencies of perception that plagued the previous incarnation of the scale. The Beaufort scale is very roughly related to the Saffir-Simpson hurricane scale, which describes hurricanes rather than slower-speed winds, and the hurricane speeds of 12 through 16 are not meant to be matched to hurricane categories. The two are related, but independent, scales.

Beaufort's weather notation was the precursor to modern weather observation codes. As he rose in rank within the navy, the frequency of Beaufort's weather observations increased, and eventually he took notes about every two hours. Beaufort's notation used the wind force number from his wind force scale, followed by a letter abbreviation that described the state of the weather and sky based on precipitation and cloud conditions. Beaufort continued to refine his system between 1806 and 1832, until the notation was adopted by the Royal Navy in 1833.

Beaufort's notation was adopted by the British Meteorological Office and approved for international exchange of weather observations at an international conference in Poland in 1935. The modern version of the scale uses numbers rather than letters and precise wind speed rather than the wind force number, although letter abbreviations are sometimes used in very specialized reports.

Admiral Beaufort died in 1857 in Sussex, England, and is buried in the church gardens of St. John at Hackney, London.

niques continue to miss the immediate onset of devastating weather events, such as tornadoes and monsoons, yet such shortcomings must be measured not against perfection, but against a baseline set by the even greater deficiencies of weather prediction methods used throughout most of human history. A warm, sunny morning in April can quickly turn to a late-spring blizzard just a few hours later; such events would have taken people by surprise just a few decades ago but are routinely predicted now, allowing people sufficient time to seek shelter.

Although hurricane and tornado prediction leave much to be desired, systems that can predict them and give advance warning just a few minutes before disaster strikes can save countless lives. In the case of an earthquake, a 60-second

Beaufort Scale

Force	WMO classification	Appearance of wind effects		Wind velocity in knots
		On the sea	On the land	
0.	CALM	Sea appears mirrorlike	Calm; smoke rises vertically	Less than 1
1.	LIGHT AIR	Small ripples, no foam crests	Gentle smoke drift indicates wind direction	1–3
2.	LIGHT BREEZE	Small wavelets appear; crests do not break	Wind felt on face, leaves rustle, vanes move	4–6
3.	GENTLE BREEZE	Larger wavelets with occasional whitecaps	Leaves and small twigs moving; light flags extended	7–10
4.	MODERATE BREEZE	Smaller waves become longer, with frequent white caps	Dust, leaves, and paper lifted; small branches move	11–16
5.	FRESH BREEZE	Larger waves form, with whitecaps and spray	Small, leafy trees begin to sway	17–21
6.	STRONG BREEZE	Whitecaps are everywhere; there is more spray	Branches of large trees sway; whistling in wires	22–27
7.	NEAR GALE	Streaking white foam appears on the back of breaking waves	Whole trees move; resistance walking into the wind	28–33
8.	GALE	Larger waves become higher, with spindrift on breaking crests and extensive foam	Whole trees move; resistance walking into the wind	34–40
9.	STRONG GALE	Sea begins to roll with high waves and heavy foam	Light structural damage (shingles blow off roofs)	41–47
10.	STORM	Very high waves occur, and the sea appears white	Considerable structural damage, trees uprooted (rare occurrence on land)	48–55
11.	VIOLENT STORM	Exceptionally high waves occur; small and medium-size ships are not visible between crests		56–63
12.	HURRICANE	Sea is completely white with driving spray; visibility is poor; the air is filled with spray		64–71
13.	HURRICANE			72–80
14.	HURRICANE			81–89
15.	HURRICANE			90–99
16.	HURRICANE			100–109
17.	HURRICANE			110–118

© Infobase Learning

The Beaufort scale classifies and describes the effects of winds at varying speeds. It became popular and has persisted in part because it combines numerical values with concise, easily understood descriptions.

warning can mean the difference between being trapped in an elevator and finding safety under a steel table.

Although weather prediction may seem to have reached a plateau, the
improvements in simulators discussed in chapter 5 do hold promise of enabling
further enhancements to weather prediction technology. A simulator is only as
good as the data on which it bases its predictions. Fortunately, today's weather
simulators are being fed an increasing diet of of increasingly varied data through
the use of better and more widespread weather sensors. Before the days of modern weather collection equipment, the weather in a particular town may have
been measured and recorded using a single thermometer located at a weather
station in the town. The town's weather history would then be recorded as a
single number or perhaps as a high and low temperature for each day of the year.
Weather predictions based on such data are inherently inaccurate because they
ignore variations in temperature that can occur within different "microclimates"
within the same town. The peak of a hill might be sunny and warm, while the
valley just a few hundred feet away at the bottom of the hill might be covered
in fog and several degrees cooler. Weather predictions based solely on average
daily temperatures within the town will fail to take such differences into account
and therefore will fail to produce highly accurate predictions. It is now becoming increasingly feasible to place larger numbers of temperature sensors into the
environment spaced more closely to each other, because the data gathered by
such sensors can be transmitted wirelessly back to weather stations quickly, with
no additional human effort and at very low cost. As more and more of these fine-
grained data are gathered throughout the world and fed into weather simulators,
such simulators will be able to produce more accurate predictions.

One can imagine that such a worldwide weather simulator, armed with
enough data, would be able to predict weather events, such as tornadoes and
floods, with great accuracy and that human meteorologists would not necessarily understand how the software formed its predictions based on the weather
history provided to it. Weather prediction software might, for example, accurately predict the occurrence of a tornado in the absence of any previous pattern
of weather events that human meteorologists associated with the formation of a
tornado. In response, the meteorologists might review the data and learn something new about how tornadoes form. On the other hand, they might be unable
to draw any conclusions and never understand how the software was able to
tease out the future occurrence of a tornado from the jumble of past events in
its database.

This is one example of what is becoming known as "data-based science," in which computers draw scientific conclusions directly from a set of data, usually a large and complex set of data, without using any process that human scientists understand. Data-based science is raising many of the same questions for science that computer-assisted proofs raise for mathematics, in particular, whether humans should ever rely on predictions or other scientific conclusions drawn by a computer if such conclusions are not verified by human scientists using accepted scientific theories. Although it is too soon to know whether or how data-based scientific conclusions will be incorporated into the body of science, both scientists and the general public will find it very difficult to reject such conclusions if they repeatedly prove accurate and capable of helping people in their everyday lives, as is the case when a data-based tornado prediction might serve as the basis for saving human lives.

7

COMPUTER-INSPIRED BIOLOGY: MAKING COMPUTERS FROM LIVING THINGS

We are all so familiar with electronic computers that one might reasonably assume that a computer *must* be electronic. In fact, modern computers often are referred to as "digital electronic computers," yet in theory, and in an increasingly wide variety of circumstances in practice, a computer does not need to be powered by or use electricity. Understanding why this is true requires revisiting what makes a computer a computer.

Recall that, at its essence, a computer consists of a "memory" and a *processor* connected to each other by a "bus." The purpose of the memory is to store software, which consists of a set of instructions. The purpose of the processor is to read the instructions from the memory and to carry out those instructions, one-by-one and in sequence. The purpose of the bus is to connect the memory to the processor, so the processor can read the instructions from the memory and optionally store results back into the memory.

In modern computers, the memory, processor, and bus take the form of electronic circuitry, and software takes the form of electrical signals stored in the memory. Computer components and software have taken this form over the last half century because electrical components can be used to implement a computer more quickly, compactly, and inexpensively than the alternatives.

A computer's memory, processor, and bus do not, however, have to be implemented using electrical circuitry. In fact, some of the earliest computing devices used purely

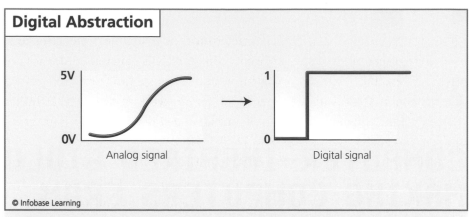

Digital Abstraction

5V

0V

Analog signal

1

0

Digital signal

© Infobase Learning

An analog signal is one whose amplitude varies continuously over time, as shown on the left. It is not possible to copy and transmit analog signals perfectly. As a result, they are not reliable for use in computers. Instead, modern computers store and transmit signals digitally to enable such storage and transmission to be performed without errors repeatedly and at high speeds. Although the lowest level of electronic components in computers use analog signals, computer circuitry interprets such analog signals as digital signals using a mechanism known as the "digital abstraction."

mechanical components to perform these functions. Charles Babbage's Analytical Engine, for example, used a variety of metal cylinders, wheels, and gears to implement the processor, memory, and bus. It used punched cards as software and also provided output (such as the results of calculations) on punched cards. Although such a computer may have been slower, less expandable, and more expensive to produce and maintain than an electronic computer, it was a computer nonetheless. In fact, the Analytical Engine was a true, general-purpose, programmable computer, whereas some of the earliest digital "computers" created in the 1940s lacked sufficient programmability to constitute true "computers" in the modern sense.

Scientists and engineers today are learning how to manipulate individual molecules as part of what is becoming known as "nanotechnology" and how to manufacture and control biological materials in what is becoming known as "bioengineering." As such techniques become more reliable and less expensive, we should expect to see computers constructed of molecules and organic matter rather than electronic circuitry constructed from silicon and metal. As the rest of this chapter explains, significant steps in this direction are already being taken.

WHAT IS DNA?

All living organisms share certain characteristics, including the presence of cells. Every living organism is made up of a collection of cells. A material inside each cell is what differentiates individual organisms and entire species from one another. This material is DNA, which is an acronym for deoxyribonucleic acid. DNA is a nucleic acid that encodes the genetic information that determines how an organism develops and grows, which is why DNA is often called "the code of life."

Working in 1969, the Swiss scientist Friedrich Miescher was the first to isolate DNA in cells. He called the substance nuclein. In the 1940s, scientists had identified the building blocks of DNA—sugar, phosphate, and four nitrogen-containing chemical bases. These bases are labeled adenine (A), cytosine (C), guanine (G), and thymine (T). Although the components of DNA were known, its structure remained a mystery until 1953. A research scientist at King's College in London, Rosalind Franklin, produced an X-ray diffraction photograph of DNA. This photograph was seen by a research team working at Cambridge University. James Watson, an American scientist, and Francis Crick, a scientist from Britain, were inspired by the photograph and their own research to propose that the DNA molecule consists of two strands arranged in a double helix. The helix resembles a spiraling ladder, with rungs connecting the two side strands.

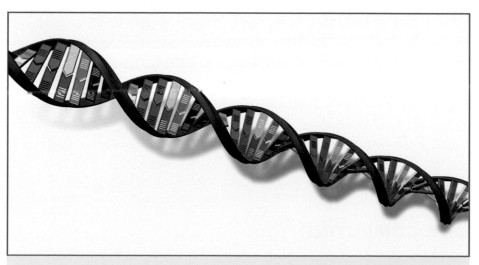

DNA (deoxyribonucleic acid) has the structure of a double helix and encodes the genetic instructions for almost all forms of life on Earth.   *(Motionstream/Shutterstock)*

Watson and Crick published their theory in the journal *Nature* in April 1953. Over the next decade, this theory became accepted as fact by other scientists. In 1962, Watson, Crick, and a colleague, Maurice Wilkins, received the Nobel Prize in physiology or medicine for their discovery. Rosalind Franklin died in 1958, and, since the Nobel Prize is never awarded posthumously, she was not recognized.

In the years since Watson and Crick announced their discovery, much has been learned about how DNA functions. The two strands that make up sides of the DNA double helix are each composed of a long chain of nucleotides. Each nucleotide consists of a deoxyribose sugar molecule that is attached to a phosphate group and one of the four nitrogen bases (A, C, G, or T). The nucleotides on each side of the helix are connected to each other by a covalent bond between a sugar from one nucleotide and a phosphate from another. The nitrogen base protrudes and is joined to a base from the other strand. The bases can be joined only according to a strict pattern: A only with T, and C only with G. These pairings are called base pairs. The base pairs make up the rungs of the DNA ladder; their sequence is called a genetic code. The sequence of the genetic code defines genetic information in the same way that letters of the alphabet can be sequenced into words.

A critical property of DNA is that it replicates, meaning that it can reproduce by making copies of itself. This occurs when cells divide. Each of the new cells receives an exact copy of the DNA that was present in the original cell. Replication is accomplished when the two strands in the DNA helix separate, with each strand serving as a template for a new strand. Through the pattern of base pair connections (with A connecting to T and C to G), two new strands are created and joined to the separated strands, forming two new double-stranded helixes of DNA. For example, given a strand with the sequence GTACAG, a new strand will be produced with the sequence CATGTC. These two strands completely replicate the original. This process, which is accomplished by an enzyme called a DNA polymerase, is the key to the inheritance of genetic traits.

DNA COMPUTING

The fields of theoretical computer science and advanced biology have given rise to the concept of DNA computing. This advanced form of computing uses DNA, molecular biology, and biochemistry to solve mathematical problems and perform other functions that are today performed by silicon-based electronic computers.

The field of DNA computing was initially proposed in 1994 by Leonard Adleman, a University of Southern California professor of computer science. Adleman became interested in doing research to find a vaccine or cure for AIDS and began to study advanced molecular biology. With a background in mathematics and theoretical computer science, he was soon struck by the similarity between the DNA polymerase and the Turing machine, a theoretical computer that was defined by the famous British mathematician Alan Turing in the 1930s. Adleman realized that just as a Turing machine could be programmed to perform the replication that is initiated by the DNA polymerase, DNA itself could be programmed to solve the same problems as the Turing machine.

A Turing machine is a simple device that consists of two components: a component (usually called "memory") for storing information and a component (usually called "processor") for performing a few simple operations that act on the information. These two components, memory and processor, are present in every computer because they are sufficient for computing anything. Adleman recognized that in DNA he had both a storage mechanism (since DNA has been storing genetic information for billions of years) that could act as a computer memory and a way to perform operations that could act as a computer processor. For Adleman, enzymes such as DNA polymerases provided evidence that DNA could be made to perform the same operations as an electronic computer.

As a proof of concept, Adleman used DNA to perform a computation known as the Hamiltonian path problem. Named for the 19th-century astronomer William Hamilton, this well-known computing problem is also known as the "traveling salesman problem." It involves finding a path from one place to another, passing through a predetermined number of points only once in the shortest possible total distance. As the number of points increases, finding the solution to the problem becomes increasingly complex. Adleman's use of DNA to solve this problem for seven points was groundbreaking because it was the first known use of DNA to perform a standard computational algorithm, which previously could be performed only by electronic computers.

In 2002, Adleman and his team of researchers used DNA computing to solve a nontrivial 20-variable 3-SAT problem that had 1 million potential solutions.

(continues on page 108)

001101010010100111010110101010101011001010000 1

Using DNA to Solve the Traveling Salesman Problem

The Traveling Salesman problem, or TSP, is one of the most extensively studied problems in computational mathematics and computer science. The concept behind the problem is relatively simple. Given a collection of cities and the cost of traveling between any two cities, what is a general method for determining the cheapest route that would take a salesman from one city to another, passing through each city once and only once? In the standard version of the problem, the cost of traveling between any two cities is the same, but some routes may allow travel in only one direction.

In the illustration, the arrows show that the salesman can travel from San Diego to Atlanta, but not in the opposite direction. Also, St. Louis cannot be one of the cities included in the solution route between two other cities because it can only be reached by passing through Atlanta more than once.

TSP is not just a fun puzzle to solve; it touches on issues related to optimization and tree spanning that are fundamental to many computer operations. The solution to TSP is deceptively simple for a small number of cities. In the illustration, it can easily be seen that a unique path exists from Boston to San Diego to Atlanta to New York. In reality, for a large number of cities, the number of routes that must be checked to find a solution increases to a very large number. Finding algorithms that work for both a small and large number of cities has been the challenge of TSP. All the algorithms that have been tried for smaller numbers of cities exhaust the resources of modern computers when applied to larger collections. In the 1970s, TSP was found by computer scientists to be "NP-complete." This means that no efficient algorithm can be found. This does not mean that no algorithms exist to solve this problem; it just means that no algorithm is known that will work efficiently with a large set of data.

When Leonard Adleman solved TSP using a DNA computer in 1994, he decided to work with a collection of seven cities and 14 one-way flight paths between the cities. He wanted to use enough data to show that the solution was nontrivial, yet the data set also needed to be small enough to work with in a biology lab. The TSP that Adleman chose had a solution that could be worked out visually by most people in less than one minute.

001101010010100111010110101010101011001010000 1

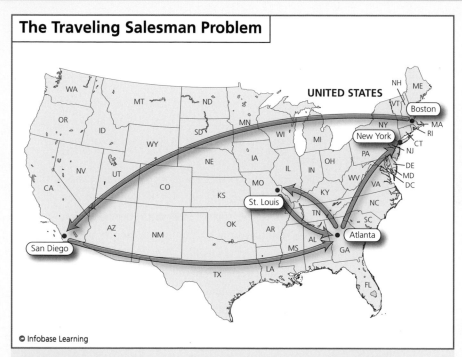

The Traveling Salesman Problem

UNITED STATES

The task of finding a path that connects all the destinations on a map, such as San Diego, Boston, New York, St. Louis, and Atlanta in this example, while passing through each destination only once and in the shortest possible total distance is known as the "traveling salesman problem." The traveling salesman problem has applications in fields such as planning, logistics, and the manufacture of microchips and often is solved using computer software.

He began by assigning a random DNA sequence (such as ACTTGCAG) to each city. He assumed that the first part of the sequence ("ACTT" in the example) stood for the name of the city (such as Atlanta). He then assumed that "flight numbers" between two cities could be described by concatenating the sequence of the origin city with the sequence of the destination city. So if New York were TCG-GACTG, then the flight between Atlanta and New York would be ACTTTCGG. At this point, Adleman turned to biology. He synthesized DNA with sequences that matched all the city names and all the flights. He combined a "pinch" (about 10^{14}

(continues)

(continued)

molecules) of each sequence in a test tube with some water, salt, and enzymes. The environment in the test tube was designed to approximate that of a cell.

With about 1/50 of a teaspoon of material in the test tub and in about one second, Adleman had the solution to the problem. During that second, trillions of molecules were interacting and replicating to perform a biological form of parallel processing. Adleman then needed to prove that at least some of the new molecules contained the solution to his TSP.

To isolate the molecules with the correct solution, Adleman used additional biochemical processes. Polymerase chain reaction (PCR) separated out the molecules with sequences that included the correct start and end cities. Another process called gel electrophoresis identified the remaining molecules with the correct length. Using a tedious process called annealing, he finally determined which molecules had sequences that supplied the solution to the problem. After the initial one-second period of DNA computation, a total of seven days in the lab were required to analyze the results. Although this process of solving TSP clearly is not about to replace today's electrical computers any time soon, it does demonstrate that, in theory, DNA can be used to solve problems programmed into it by humans.

(continued from page 105)

A SAT problem involves the concept of satisfiability. The problem is solved by determining how a given set of variables can be assigned such that a Boolean formula evaluates to "true" (is satisfied). The team used a procedure similar to the one Adleman used for his original proof of concept in 1994. They began by synthesizing a mixture of DNA strands to simulate the solution space of the problem. Biochemical techniques were then used to perform algorithms on the strands and eliminate those that brought incorrect results. Finally, the strands that were left represented the solution to the problem, as shown by analysis of the nucleotide sequences of the remaining strands.

Adleman's original work on DNA computing led the way to further developments. In 2002, researchers led by Tom Ran and Ehud Shapiro at the Weizmann Institute of Science in Israel announced their creation of a programmable molecular computer built from DNA molecules and enzymes. In 2009, they announced that the computer was able to run simple logic programs, similar to those executed by electronic computers. Professor Shapiro has stated that the ultimate goal of this type of computer is the development of independent programmable computing devices that operate in a biological environment. The team has already demonstrated another DNA computer that is able to diagnose cancerous activity within a cell and release an anticancer drug.

Another research effort led by Tom Knight of MIT has developed the concept of BioBricks, which are standard DNA sequences that encode basic biological functions. BioBricks are defined by a common interface and are an attempt to introduce engineering practices and standards into the field of synthetic biology. The BioBricks Foundation, which was formed by Knight and other researchers from MIT, Harvard, and the University of California at San Francisco maintains a library of BioBricks that can be used to construct biological computing structures. According to the BioBricks Foundation Web site, "Using BioBrick™ standard biological parts, a synthetic biologist or biological engineer can already, to some extent, program living organisms in the same way a computer scientist can program a computer."

THE BENEFITS OF DNA COMPUTING

One of the most significant potential benefits of DNA computing is that, at least in theory, very large numbers of DNA molecules could be used to perform computations simultaneously—"in parallel"—thereby significantly increasing the speed with which such computations could be carried out in comparison to traditional computers, which typically perform only one computation at a time—"in series." This particular form of "parallel processing" could be especially useful for solving problems that require using a single set of rules to evaluate a very large number of possibilities. A perfect example of such a problem is the traveling salesman problem discussed above, in which each of a very large number of possible travel routes must be evaluated against the same two criteria—the total length of the path traveled along the route and whether any city on the route is visited more than once. DNA computers could potentially solve such problems thousands of times faster than traditional electronic computers.

For example, because more than 10 trillion DNA molecules can fit into a single cubic centimeter (less than 0.1 cubic inch), a DNA computer that fit within this space could potentially perform 10 trillion computations simultaneously. The magnitude of such an achievement can be understood by considering that today's *microprocessor* manufacturers, such as Intel, often spend on the order of a $1 billion to design and manufacture a new processor that is only two or three times faster than the previous year's model.

Another benefit of DNA computing is that it consumes much less power per computation than traditional silicon-based electronic computers. This feature is particularly attractive in light of worldwide efforts to reduce the total amount of power consumed by computers as their numbers grow. Furthermore, at least with respect to certain kinds of computational tasks, DNA computers can be smaller than silicon-based computers of comparable computing power. Silicon-based computer processors appear to be reaching their physical limits of speed and miniaturization. As a result, researchers are working hard to determine whether DNA computers may provide a viable way to continue to increase the speed and decrease the size of computers once it becomes impossible to continue doing so using silicon-based electronic computers.

Yet another potential advantage of DNA computers is that their construction would not necessarily involve the use of toxic materials of the kind normally used in the manufacture of electronic devices. The use of such toxic materials poses health risks to those who work in plants that manufacture electronic devices and to the general public when a computing device is disposed of improperly. In contrast, because DNA computers would be constructed from organic materials, the proponents of DNA computing argue that DNA computers would not necessarily contain any toxic substances and could be disposed of safely.

THE CHALLENGES OF DNA COMPUTING

Although the description above might make it seem that DNA computers are ready to roll off the department store shelves and into offices tomorrow, DNA computing still faces significant challenges that it must overcome if it is ever to serve as the basis for computers that are useful anywhere except in laboratories as academic curiosities. For example, although Leonard Adleman was able to use DNA to solve the traveling salesman problem, doing so took days of work, including manual effort by Adleman, to extract the results. This is the equivalent of performing a calculation on a personal computer, only to require connecting an oscilloscope and performing a series of experiments on the computer's circuitry to discover the result of the calculation produced by the computer. Although such a process might be acceptable to a professional scientist, especially if there were no other way available to solve the same problem, DNA computers must become faster and more automated if they are to become suitable for widespread use in universities, businesses, governments, and homes.

Furthermore, the problems that DNA has been used to solve so far have used particular strands of DNA selected for their suitability in solving particular problems. The same DNA could not be used to solve other problems. In other words, no one has yet developed a general-purpose programmable computer constructed from DNA that could be programmed to solve any problem in the same way that any modern electronic computer can be programmed to run any software. To construct a truly general-purpose programmable DNA computer would first require designing and building reliable DNA-based versions of the fundamental building blocks of computers, known as "logic gates," and then constructing larger components from those building blocks. Although there have been some initial successes at building DNA-based logic gates, these initial prototypes are neither very reliable nor capable of being combined together in large enough numbers to serve as the basis for a useful computer.

In fact, it is not clear whether it will ever be possible to construct a DNA computer that can compete with an electronic computer in terms of size and flexibility. There might be inherent or practical limits on the ways that DNA can be combined together to work as components of a human-programmable computer. At this point, the field of DNA computing is too young to know the answer to this question. Even if, however, DNA computers are limited to solving only a certain kind of problem, they may still prove useful to scientists if their ability to perform computations in parallel allows them to solve such problems more quickly than their electronic cousins.

OBJECTIONS TO DNA COMPUTING

Many people have an immediate, intuitive negative reaction to DNA computing because it involves manipulating the materials of life for use as machines. The term *DNA computing* conjures up images of enslaving humans or animals and hooking them up to computers so their bodies can be used to perform computations against their wills. One objection to DNA computing backs up this gut reaction with the argument that no part of a living organism, no matter how small, should be used as a machine. According to this argument, life is simply off limits for use as a computer or part of a computer. This argument may be backed by reference to religious doctrine or nonreligious ethical theory about the sanctity of life and the prohibition against using any living being, particularly a human being, merely as a means to an end. In this view, DNA computing should be completely prohibited for all the same reasons that human slavery is completely prohibited, no matter how beneficial it might be to slave owners.

Even those who do not object to DNA computing on moral grounds find other objections. One is the purely pragmatic objection that DNA computing will never be capable of producing reliable, large-scale, general-purpose computers that will be able to compete with today's electronic computers. According to this argument, the fact that DNA has been used successfully to solve a few problems, such as the traveling salesman problem, very slowly and under highly constrained conditions, does not imply that it will ever become possible to construct a DNA computer that can be programmed with a large and complex computer program to perform any function desired by the programmer in the way today's electronic computers can be programmed. Even if DNA computing is made more reliable, some argue that DNA will be capable only of performing a limited range of tasks using specialized equipment and skill and that the term *computer* should therefore not even apply to DNA because it will not be capable of general-purpose programming.

Yet another objection to DNA computing is that because we have only a limited understanding of how DNA works and because we have even less understanding of how human-programmed DNA might work, we should not further develop DNA computing technology because by doing so we risk releasing programmed DNA into the environment, with potentially devastating impacts on humans and other naturally existing life forms. One concern is that programmed DNA could infect people and cause illness or death or that, even worse, programmed DNA could begin to replicate (copy itself) without limit, swallowing everything in its path and thereby creating what technologist Bill Joy called a "gray goo" that would overrun the planet. Although such an extreme scenario may be unlikely, it points

`1001110100101010100110010111011010100101001`

Tom Knight, MIT Computer Science Professor and Pioneer in Using Biological Materials to Perform Computations

Tom Knight arrived at the Massachusetts Institute of Technology (MIT) as a 10th-grade student in 1963 and remains there as a senior research scientist in the Computer Science and Artificial Intelligence Laboratory. Although his early years were spent doing traditional computer science and building hardware, his later interests and current work lie in the area of synthetic biology, that is, using biological materials for computations.

In his early days at MIT, in 1967, Knight wrote the original kernel for the ITS operating system. He designed one of the first semiconductor memory-based bitmap displays as well as the MIT Lisp Machine processor. He also worked on the design and implementation of the first local area network on the MIT campus in 1975. Knight's accomplishments also include the creation of the first silicon retina in 1981 and the single-chip optical mouse. He became interested in biological sys-

The MIT professor Tom Knight, a leading researcher in the field of synthetic biology, is shown here holding vials of BioBricks, which are standard DNA sequences that encode basic biological functions. *(Gary H. Anthes/Computerworld)*

tems in the 1990s, partly inspired by the work of Harold Morowitz of Yale University. Knight set up a biology lab within the CSAIL, which aims to create standard biological parts and assembly techniques in order to build and test functional biological systems, or living cells. The lab is currently using the *E. coli* K-12 bacterium,

(continues)

`1001110100101010100110010111011010100101001`

(continued)

which has been sequenced and annotated and is in the process of being reduced and standardized from its original 4,000 genes in order to create a manageable basis for biological engineering.

Knight seeks to bridge the concepts of biology and engineering in his work. Engineers are taught to reduce everything to the simplest forms possible in order to find a solution, while biologists study the complexity of natural systems. Knight observes that natural systems have many built-in redundancies, which makes them more flexible and resilient than human-made machinery. He seeks to develop a new generation of computers that would mimic natural systems in flexibility and would be cheap to manufacture. However, his ultimate goal is to be able to program bacteria in a way that one can program a microprocessor, with the ability to turn individual genes on and off, to add or remove new ones, and to be able to generally manipulate the life cycle and evolution process.

to the more general risks of tampering with the building blocks of life in ways that could have negative consequences that we cannot predict. Although European countries tend to adopt what is known as the "precautionary principle" toward DNA computing and other untested technologies, according to which such technologies are not to be commercialized or released to the public unless and until those who develop them have proven that they are safe, the United States tends to adopt the opposite approach, according to which new materials can be marketed unless they have been demonstrated to cause harm.

CONCLUSIONS

For most of the history of both computer science and biology, the two fields have followed distinct paths. Computer science originally developed out of a combination of the abstract discipline of mathematics, the "hard" science of physics, and electrical engineering. The process of creating computer software has been considered to be driven primarily by rules of logic and principles of engineering design. Computer scientists traditionally create software by writing programs according to the rules of programming languages and then running the software merely to verify that it works as designed. Biology, in contrast, has traditionally been considered a "soft" science, governed by observation of the natural world and experimentation. Biologists tend to develop categories of organisms according to their shared histories and functional relationships, not by mathematical formulas. Furthermore, biologists typically have not had the tools necessary to "design" new organisms in the same way that software developers design software by writing code. Instead, biologists have played a role in creating new life forms using techniques based mainly on trial-and-error experiments, such as by breeding different species of plants together and observing the properties of the resulting offspring.

Over time, however, biologists gradually learned that the building blocks of life have more in common with computer hardware and software than was first realized. The DNA in each cell of an organism contains instructions for constructing the organism's cells, much as computer memory stores software. The process by which organisms use DNA to grow and differentiate cells is analogous to the way in which computer processors carry out software instructions. In other words, the natural processes carried out by DNA mirror those performed by computers. Once biologists and computer scientists realized this, they recognized that, at least in theory, it might be possible to intentionally program DNA to perform functions designed into it by humans rather than the functions it performs naturally, and that in doing so DNA could be made into a biological computer that runs organic software.

Although biological computing is still in its infancy, the promise it holds has sparked great interest among both computer scientists and biologists to learn more about each others' fields. As a result of these and other developments, small pockets of biology are becoming more like traditional computer science, incorporating rules of logic, design, and programming. Predesigned biological building blocks can already be purchased for use in constructing made-to-order DNA sequences. This shift from biology as soft science to biology as hard engineering is just one of many transitions in the theory and practice of discovery and invention that are being brought about using computers.

8

BIOLOGY-INSPIRED COMPUTING: LEARNING FROM NATURE

Humans long have studied nature for the purpose of incorporating structures and processes from nature into human artifacts and techniques. Early builders copied arched cave entrances to design arches in the doorways of their homes, while early hunters mimicked stalking tigers to catch their prey. However, such adherence to natural forms has often been rejected by modern scientists and engineers largely as a result of some significant failures of this approach and spectacular successes achieved by inventing structures that bear little or no resemblance to those that exist in nature. Early manned flying machines that copied the wing structure of birds led to embarrassing failures and often to the deaths of their inventors. Engineers achieved human flight only by designing machines whose wings and other components bore little resemblance to those in nature. The airplane is just one of many examples that demonstrate that nature's solution to a problem at a particular scale (such as at the scale of a sparrow) cannot necessarily be applied at a much larger scale (such as at the scale of a human). A house of 52 cards is sturdy, but a house of 1,000 cards collapses under its own weight.

Despite the successes of scientific and engineering techniques that bear little resemblance to those found in the natural world, such techniques can themselves reach their limits. Although the Internet was designed to be resilient against attack, the defense mechanisms created to protect it when it consisted of only a few thousand computers in government agencies and universities have been surpassed in a world in which the Internet now includes millions of computers embedded in everything from cell phones to automobile navigation systems. Disaster plans that were developed to provide emergency medical services in small towns may break down when applied to a metropolis in the wake of a natural disaster or epidemic.

As a result of these and other limitations to traditional forms of scientific problem solving, innovators have begun to look once again to nature's complex and often elegant solutions to difficult problems, such as how to ward off a virus, how to heal an injured body, and how to convert sunlight efficiently into energy. This chapter explores just a few of the ways in which computer scientists, in particular, are turning to biology for their inspiration.

LIMITATIONS OF TRADITIONAL COMPUTERS

The processing power of computers has increased exponentially for decades according to what has become known as "Moore's law," named for the Intel engineer Gordon Moore. According to one version of Moore's law, the amount of processing power that can be purchased for a dollar doubles every 18 months. To get a sense of just how quickly computers improve according to this law, consider that a computer that cost $100,000 in 1980 would have cost only $25,000 in 1983, $6,250 in 1985, $3,125 in 1987, and less than $100 in 2010—a 99.9 percent decrease in price in just 30 years. Another way to view the same improvement is that the same $100,000 would buy a computer in 2010 that is 1,000 times more powerful than the same amount of money would have bought in 1980.

With such massive advances in computer technology, one might wonder whether today's computers have any limitations and whether there are any problems they cannot solve. Even so, modern computers, as impressive as they may be in comparison to their counterparts from just a few years ago, still lack even a fraction of the capabilities needed to accurately predict the weather more than a few days in advance, decipher the boom and bust cycles of modern economies, and determine whether a new drug will have undesirable chemical reactions in any part of the human body. Solving such problems requires keeping track of such a large amount of data representing such a high number of interacting variables that to attempt to use a computer to examine all such possibilities could take thousands of years. One reason modern computers continue to have such difficulty with these types of problems is that they are limited to carrying out one instruction at a time in sequence, whereas these problems inherently involve events that occur simultaneously and in parallel (such as many traders buying and selling stocks simultaneously in a stock market, whereby each trade affects future stock prices, which in turn affects future trades).

Computers that could mimic the nature of such problems by carrying out multiple instructions in parallel would be capable of solving such problems more quickly and possibly more accurately than serial computers. Although much work has been done in recent years to make computers with parallel processing hardware (such as the "dual quad" processors popular in many computers today), such hardware typically contains only a small number of processors working together, and the software that runs on such hardware typically is not specifically designed for use on parallel processors. As a result, parallel processing hardware usually does not achieve as much of an increase in speed as one might expect. In contrast, living organisms almost always perform multiple tasks simultaneously. A tree simultaneously converts sunlight into chlorophyll, transports water from roots into leaves, and produces sap. The DNA in millions

An Allegory: Software CEO Meets Automobile CEO

The following joke may be found in various forms on the Internet. At a computer tradeshow a few years ago, Bill Gates compared the computer and automobile industries. "If General Motors kept up with technology at the same pace as the computer industry over the past 30 years, cars would cost $25 and get 1,000 miles per gallon." The CEO of GM quickly fired back in a press release, "That may be true, but who would want to drive a car that crashes twice a day?"

This joke has become "viral" because it carries a germ of truth. While there have been amazing advances in computer technology over the past few decades, many computer systems still exhibit serious reliability problems. Some of these problems are related to computer hardware, but the majority can be attributed to quality issues of computer software. As more people have begun to use computers and products with embedded software and as more industries have been automated with computer systems, the dependability of software has become critically important.

Many software quality problems are related to complexity and scale. The world has become more dependent on large-scale and complex software systems. Even the operating systems that run PCs are very complex pieces of software compared to 10 or 20 years ago. Large-scale software systems can extend to hundreds of

of cells in an organism replicates simultaneously. A person can carry on a conversation with a friend while driving a car (requiring processing visual, tactile, and auditory information and manipulating the steering wheel and pedals using hands and feet) while subconsciously remembering the name of a friend who was mentioned an hour earlier. If computers could be designed to incorporate some of these abilities of biological organisms, they might become capable of solving complex problems more quickly.

Furthermore, computers are notoriously prone to bugs that cause them to crash. Even an error in a single bit of a large piece of software (i.e., a 0 that should be a 1, or vice versa) can bring the entire computer crashing to a halt. This might be analogized to a person dying as a result of a single hair falling out. People and other living things can continue to function not only after small malfunctions

thousands and even millions of lines of code. Adding to the complexity is the fact that many software systems are based on older "legacy" programs that were implemented at a time when the standards of reliability were less demanding. Testing and maintaining complex, large-scale, and legacy-based systems usually requires large teams of software engineers whose work must be precisely defined and coordinated.

Many software systems must perform the same operations repeatedly, sometimes millions of times per second and often over an extended period. Software systems are required to run on hardware that is unforgiving and sometimes prone to errors of its own. Given these requirements, software engineers must anticipate all types of failures and include contingency operations in the software to handle them.

Software reliability is one of the most important and rapidly growing areas of software development. Any organization that implements a large-scale software system must establish processes to test, measure, and assess the reliability of the software. Since even a minor typing error in a line of code can result in software failure, software development organizations must find and fix as many problems as possible before releasing software for public use. This is especially critical for software systems in which errors can result in loss of human life or some other form of catastrophe.

(such as catching a cold or stubbing a toe) but also even after suffering serious injury. If such robustness in the face of adverse conditions could be imported into computers, then computers would need far less service and support and would last longer without needing to be replaced.

In addition, computers do an excellent job at following the instructions they have been given in the form of software but not at creating new instructions to follow. In contrast, even a small child can learn from his or her environment and adapt to it, such as by learning not to touch a fire after being burned. Entire species adapt to the natural environment through the process of biological evolution. If even a small amount of this flexibility and ability to learn could be integrated into computers, they could be used in a wider variety of circumstances without the need for human programmers to modify them to do so. For these and other reasons, computer scientists have increasingly been turning to the natural world for inspiration in designing the next generation of computer hardware and software, which is what the remainder of this chapter explores.

ARTIFICIAL NEURAL NETWORKS

People have always been drawn to viewing computers as "electronic brains." It therefore should not be surprising that computer scientists who look to the natural world for inspiration in designing software should look to the human brain as a model. The brains of animals consist of a large number of cells called neurons that are interconnected with one another in a vast electrochemical network. As a result, computer software modeled on the human brain operates using what is known as an "artificial neural network" (ANN).

Traditional computer software has knowledge "hardwired" into it. For example, a typical computer program for determining how to schedule meetings among large groups of people most efficiently will contain scheduling rules that were written by human programmers. When running, the software will carry out these preprogrammed rules. Although such software may be capable of performing impressive feats, such as finding a way to schedule 20 meetings among 100 people in the course of a week in a way that minimizes the amount of time participants spend traveling, the software will not improve over time. Because it merely follows the rules provided to it, the software cannot *learn*.

In contrast, software that employs an artificial neural network can learn over time in a way roughly analogous to how the brain acquires new information and

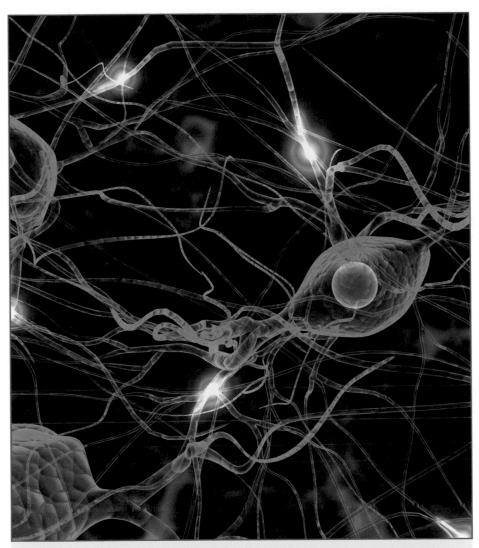

A neuron, also known as a nerve cell, contains a cell body (also known as the soma), dendrites extending from the cell body, and an axon. Neurons attach to each other at connections called synapses, across which neurons transmit electrical and/or chemical signals.   *(Sebastian Kaulitzki/Shutterstock)*

develops problem-solving skills. For example, to use an ANN to schedule meetings, the network must first be "trained" by "showing" it a large number of meeting schedules and, for each one, telling the neural network whether the schedule is efficient. Based on this "training data," the neural network gradually "learns" what distinguishes an efficient schedule from one that wastes many people's time. The more training data provided to the neural network, the more accurate the conclusions it can draw. This kind of "training by example" is analogous to the way in which both animals and humans learn to avoid touching fires and other hot objects; by touching many different types of objects, being burned by some and not by others, and thereby learning which objects to avoid touching in the future. A well-designed ANN, like a person, can learn not only to recognize previously seen cases, but to interpolate and extrapolate from them to new cases, just as a person who has been burned by a small fire can conclude that a larger fire will also burn without needing to touch it first.

ANNs are particularly useful for recognizing patterns and for drawing conclusions based on data that cannot be processed according to simple rules. For example, consider "optical character recognition," which is the process of converting an image of a page of text into the individual letters of the text. As a particularly simple case, imagine that the word "hello" has been written on paper using a pencil and then scanned into a computer. The resulting image consists of a two-dimensional grid of black and white dots, known as "pixels," that, when viewed from a distance, represent the handwritten word "Hello." One might think it would be easy to write software that could recognize such an image as the letter "H," followed by the letter "e," and so on. For example, one might write a rule telling the software that whenever it sees two parallel vertical lines connected at their midsections by a horizontal line, it should interpret such a shape as the letter "H."

In practice, however, such rules perform very poorly at recognizing text because they fail to take into account all the ways in which the letter "H" can appear without following the rule. Someone with sloppy handwriting might write an "H" using three curved lines rather than straight lines, or without connecting all the lines to one another, or by using two lines rather than three. A simple rule will fail to recognize all of these as the letter "H," even though a human would immediately recognize the "H" in each case. This is a case in which an ANN that has been trained using thousands of "H"s written by hundreds of different people can learn to see the similarity in all the "H"s despite their differences and in the absence of a bright-line rule that distinguishes the letter "H" from other letters. Although an ANN may make mistakes, particularly if it is shown a new letter "H" that falls too far outside its prior "experience" (represented by the training data that was provided to it), it can provide significant improvements over rule-based systems.

Neural networks are useful not only for enabling computers to perform tasks that would be highly tedious to define by rules but also for solving problems that cannot be solved using any rules known to humans. For example, ANNs are often used for detecting the onset of dangerous conditions in facilities such as nuclear power plants and oil refineries. Although some of these conditions can be identified using known rules, such as the rule that a nuclear reactor core should be shut down if it exceeds a particular temperature, other conditions are not as easy to identify. For example, it might turn out that the reactor is prone to meltdown even when the core temperature is still low if some unusual combination of high air pressure, low water temperature, and high humidity occurs. Although it might be difficult or impossible for human engineers to predict in advance that such a confluence of factors would pose a danger, an ANN trained using a history of conditions that have caused problems in the reactor might be able to identify such conditions as problematic and thereby signal a warning before they occur.

For similar reasons, ANNs have proven useful in controlling robots to interact with new environments, scanning images to identify abnormalities (such as a tumor in an X-ray or a potential nuclear weapons facility in a satellite image) and to recognize previously seen patterns (such as recognizing a face in a crowd based on a driver's license photograph), and protecting computer networks against attack. Because neural networks learn to solve problems by processing large amounts of historical data, they are gaining increasing interest from scientists as larger amounts of data become available in electronic form in every field. For example, the rise of electronic medical records means that an increasing amount of information about current medical conditions and patient histories is now available in computer databases. Although the most immediate benefits of maintaining such information in electronic form is that doing so enables individual doctors to treat individual patients more efficiently and effectively, such information could also be provided to an ANN to identify previously unknown linkages between diseases and their causes. Such newfound knowledge could then be used to spot symptoms of diseases early so that they could be treated or even prevented. This is just one example of how existing electronic information, which may have been created solely to save paper and reduce costs, could serve as the basis for new knowledge gained using ANNs.

EVOLUTIONARY COMPUTATION

Biological evolution, through what is sometimes called "natural selection" by "survival of the fittest," has proven itself capable of producing species that can survive in nearly every natural environment. It is possible to view biological evolution as a problem-solving method that has overcome such dilemmas as, "What kind of breathing mechanism is necessary for surviving a mile beneath the surface of ocean?," "How can a plant store enough water to survive in the middle of a desert?," and "How should a pair of legs be constructed to evade a cheetah?" Soon after computers were invented, computer scientists began to wonder whether it might be possible to program a computer to solve problems using the same basic algorithm as biological evolution. The result is a growing field of computer science known as "evolutionary computation."

To understand how evolutionary computation works, consider an example in which a human antenna designer uses evolutionary computation software to design an antenna that weighs less than an ounce and is capable of transmitting FM radio signals smoothly (without variations in signal amplitude). The first step is for the designer to create software that can simulate the basic steps of biological evolution. Many such pieces of software now exist, so that people who wish to use evolutionary computation to solve new problems do not need to create their own software from scratch.

The next, and arguably most important, step is for the antenna designer to define a "fitness function" that specifies the features desired in the antenna being sought. In this case, the fitness function would specify that the ideal antenna would weigh less than one ounce and be capable of transmitting radio signals within the FM radio frequency spectrum. Such a fitness function must, of course, be written in a suitable language that the evolutionary computation software can understand.

The antenna designer must also specify an artificial genome that essentially defines the features that can vary from antenna to antenna. For example, the genome might specify that an antenna must be constructed of metal but that the choice of metal can vary, that an antenna must consist of straight-line segments but that the number of segments, their lengths, and their angles can vary, and so forth. This is analogous to specifying that a mammal must have lungs, skin, a spine, and fur but that the details of such characteristics can vary from mammal to mammal.

The evolutionary computation software then begins simulating evolution, first by generating an initial "population" of possible antennas that fall within the range of variations specified by the artificial genome defined earlier by the antenna designer. For example, the software might randomly generate 500 antennas made out of different metals that have different numbers of segments and segments connected at different angles to each other. This is analogous to the initial life forms that emerged out of the primordial ooze on Earth billions of years ago.

The evolutionary computation software then simulates the performance of the antennas, such as by mimicking the transmission of radio signals of varying frequencies through the antennas using a physics simulator. The software evaluates the antennas' performance using the fitness function defined earlier by the engineer. Recall that the fitness function called for an antenna that weighs less than one ounce and is capable of transmitting FM radio signals. The software evaluates each antenna in the initial population and ranks it according to its weight and ability to transmit FM radio signals. Lightweight antennas capable of transmitting FM signals without varying amplitudes receive the highest scores.

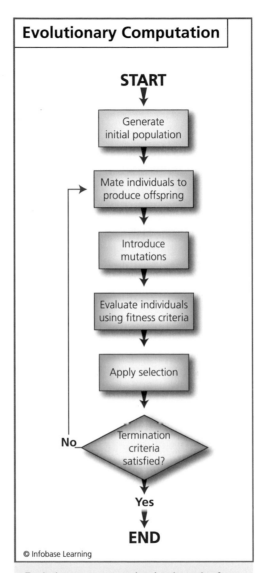

© Infobase Learning

Evolutionary computation is a branch of computer science that attempts to solve computational problems using processes inspired by biological evolution in the natural world.

Next, the software removes low-scoring antennas from the population. This simulates the death of organisms in the real world that are unfit for survival, such as organisms in the desert that require a constant supply of water to survive.

The software might also combine features from one antenna with another—such as the choice of metal from one with the choice of segments from another—to produce an "offspring" antenna to add to the population. Finally, the software might introduce some random variation into some of the offspring, such as adding an additional random segment, to simulate the process of mutation in the natural world.

The software then repeats all the steps above for the new population of antennas by simulating their behavior, evaluating how well they perform, weeding out low performers, and producing offspring (possibly with mutations) to produce yet another "generation" of antennas. The software might repeat this process for hundreds or thousands of generations. The result, if all the initial conditions were set up correctly and with a bit of luck, will be a generation of simulated antennas that are very low in weight and highly suitable for transmitting FM radio signals. In short, the evolutionary computation software produces such antennas using the same basic process by which biological evolution produces species that are fit to survive in their natural environments. The major difference between the two is that biological evolution operates according to the real-world laws of nature, while evolutionary computation is guided by artificial laws of nature provided to it by humans.

Evolutionary computation has been used successfully to solve problems ranging from scheduling large fleets of vehicles so as to optimize the use of time and fuel, to designing new drugs, to controlling the operation of fuel refineries. Evolutionary computation is growing in popularity as a problem-solving technique as the underlying algorithms improve and as the powerful computer hardware needed to effectively run evolutionary computation software grows increasingly available at lower and lower prices. Evolutionary algorithms are particularly well suited for use by scientists interested in exploring a range of possibilities quickly, even if they do not know what form those possibilities might take ahead of time.

ARTIFICIAL IMMUNE SYSTEMS AND AUTONOMIC COMPUTING

Although plants and animals have evolved a wide variety of adaptations for surviving in their natural environments, no organism is perfect. Every living thing is subject to attack by predators, infection by disease, and injury by accident, among other calamities. Any creature that did not have mechanisms for surviving such adversities would not live long.

Organisms in the natural world protect themselves against and recover from some of these kinds of damage using immune systems. Although most people who come down with a cold take some kind of medicine to ease the symptoms, the immune system of a healthy person typically rids the body of the cold in three to five days, even in the absence of medicine and despite the fact that the so-called common cold can be caused by any of hundreds of viruses. Once recovered from a cold, the previously sick person's body returns to normal functioning. The immune system has achieved its goal: to keep the body in a state of homeostasis, a steady state of operation in which all body systems function smoothly and within narrow limits (such as maintenance of the core body temperature at roughly 98.6°F [37°C]).

Natural immune systems protect the body not only from viruses but also from bacteria, fungi, and parasites. Although immune systems use a wide variety of mechanisms to cast off invaders, all such mechanisms must be capable of distinguishing between the body's own cells and cells that do not belong to the body. If the immune system incorrectly concludes that the body's own cells are outsiders, the immune system attacks those cells; in effect, the body will attack itself. Conversely, if the immune system fails to recognize invasive cells as such, it will fail to take action, thereby potentially allowing the body to succumb to disease. A healthy body with a well-functioning immune system "knows" which cells are its own and takes quick action against harmful cells from the outside, such as by sending white blood cells to attack bacteria.

Computer systems can experience problems that are analogous to infectious diseases. Although the example that probably comes immediately to mind is a computer virus that infects one or more systems, computers are also subject to damage from electrical power spikes, wear and tear on electrical and mechanical components, and changes in temperature and humidity. The effects of these events on the computer's hardware and software are similar in many ways to the effects of disease on the body of an animal. In response to this recognition, computer scientists developed the concept of an "artificial immune system" as a way to use some of the knowledge gained about how natural immune systems work to improve the ability of computers to protect themselves against "disease" and to heal themselves.

Natural immune systems have several properties that make them desirable as models for computerized immune systems. For example, natural immune systems consist of many autonomous components. As a result, the immune system can continue to fight disease even if one of the immune system's components proves ineffective or breaks down. As another example, natural immune systems can learn from new infections to fight them more effectively the next time they are encountered.

Like natural immune systems, artificial immune systems attempt to distinguish between "self" and "nonself." In the context of antivirus software that uses an artificial immune system, this means distinguishing between software that has been intentionally installed on the computer by its user (self) and software that has installed itself on the computer (nonself). Once the latter software is identified, it can be scanned for viruses or handled in other ways to ensure that it does not harm the computer. Just as in the real world, it can be particularly difficult to accurately distinguish between self and nonself in all cases in such a system, particularly when attempting to determine whether software that the system has never encountered before should be treated as a threat. One way to make such a distinction is to identify patterns in software that are already known to be harmless (such as the operating system) and patterns in software that are already known to be harmful (such as known viruses) and then to search for both types of patterns in new software to evaluate the likelihood that it is "nonself" and therefore potentially harmful.

Closely related to artificial immune systems is the concept of *autonomic computing*. It takes its name from an initiative launched by IBM in 2001 and is capable of managing and modifying itself automatically based on human-defined policies. As a simple example, a human system administrator might tell an autonomic computer that hard disk drives in the system should never be more than 80 percent full. In response to this instruction, the computer system would monitor all of its hard drives and, upon detecting a hard drive at more than 80 percent of capacity, transfer some of that data to another drive to keep all drives in the system at less than the limit set by the policy. Currently, such policies are typically enforced manually by human system administrators. As this example illustrates, an autonomic computer system would be capable of regulating itself automatically, thereby improving performance of the system, reducing the likelihood of crashes and other malfunctions, and significantly reducing the amount of human maintenance required.

Some believe that as computer systems grow increasingly large, interconnected, and complex, autonomic computing will become not only beneficial but also necessary because computer systems will become too complex to be managed by humans. The difficulty that security experts have in keeping up with new viruses launched every day provides some evidence that automatically self-managed computers will be needed if tomorrow's computer systems are not to collapse under the weight of their own size and complexity.

SIMULATED ANNEALING

Many problems in science and engineering involve finding a minimum value of an equation or other mathematical function. For example, when designing the frame of an airplane wing, it is desirable to find a shape that minimizes the drag on the wing so that it can move through the air as efficiently as possible. It can be extremely difficult to find the right wing shape by experimental trial and error because the number of possible shapes is so large that there is not enough time, money, materials, and other resources to try them all. The job is made easier if one knows the mathematical relationship between the quantity to be minimized—such as air drag—and the variables that define the shape of the wing—such as its width, length, and curvature. Even when such a relationship can be defined by an equation or other mathematical function, however, it is often not possible to simply derive the combination of variables that produces the minimum air drag. Instead, in most cases, it is necessary to "search" for the minimum air drag by trying different combinations of width, height, and curvature, observing their effects on air drag, and then picking the combination that produces the lowest drag.

Because the number of possible combinations is so large, however, it is usually not feasible to try them all. As a result, the best one can do is search through a small subset of possibilities as efficiently as possible in a way that maximizes the likelihood of finding the one that produces the true minimum possible air drag. Mathematicians and scientists have developed many such techniques that attempt to find the "global minimum" of a mathematical function.

One potential problem with all such techniques is that they can get "stuck" in what is known as a "local minimum" and therefore fail to find the true global minimum of the variable whose minimum value is desired. As an analogy, imagine attempting to find the lowest point in a vast mountain range merely by hiking

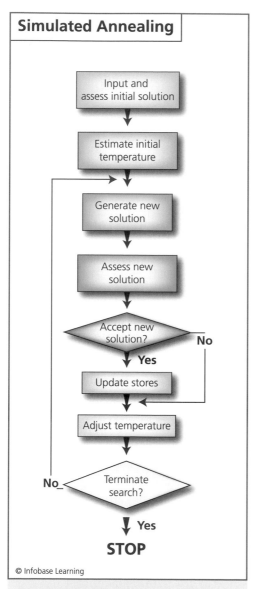

Simulated Annealing

Input and assess initial solution

↓

Estimate initial temperature

↓

Generate new solution

↓

Assess new solution

↓

Accept new solution? **No**

↓ **Yes**

Update stores

↓

Adjust temperature

↓

No Terminate search?

↓ **Yes**

STOP

© Infobase Learning

Simulated annealing is a process carried out by computers to search for the solution to a problem in a manner that mimics the natural process of annealing in metals.

through it. The only tools you have are your own eyes (which cannot see through mountains or very far into the distance) and an altimeter (a device that tells you how high you are). You walk up and down various mountain peaks and finally reach a very low point. You look all around you and can see only points on the ground that are higher than you. Can you be confident that you have found the lowest point in the entire mountain range? How can you be sure that there is not a lower point just out of view, beyond a mountain peak that is blocking it from sight? Although you might think you have found the *global* minimum, instead you might be standing on a *local* minimum—a point that is lower than any other in its immediate vicinity but not the lowest in the entire mountain range. Just as it is tempting to declare that you have found the global minimum of the mountain range as soon as you stumble upon a point that appears lowest from your vantage point, so, too, can automated techniques get stuck in a local minimum and become incapable of finding the true global minimum.

Simulated annealing is one automated technique for finding an approximation of the global minimum of a mathematical function. Its name stems from the fact that it operates by analogy to annealing in metals, a process involving heating and cooling a metal to increase the size of its crystals and reduce the number of defects it contains. Heating the metal releases its atoms from their original locations, causing them to float randomly. Cooling the metal increases the likelihood that the freed atoms will fall into configurations with lower internal energy and therefore fewer defects than their original configurations. The end result is that the atoms in the metal settle into an overall lower energy state, much like finding a global minimum.

The major advantage of simulated annealing over other techniques for finding a global minimum is that it is less likely to get stuck in a local minimum because it has the ability to "climb" out of a local minimum, thereby increasing the likelihood that it will find an even lower point if one exists. Certain other techniques will never attempt to climb to a higher point as a way of reaching a lower point. As a result, although such techniques may reach a conclusion more quickly than simulated annealing, the conclusions they reach are more likely to be inaccurate.

Whether to use simulated annealing or some other technique for finding a global minimum depends largely on the situation for which the minimum is being sought. For example, a physics simulator for use in a videogame might not need to model the flight of objects through the air with extremely high accuracy, only with enough accuracy to produce relatively realistic looking animations. In such a case, a fast but relatively inaccurate algorithm for finding a local minimum might be sufficient. In contrast, when designing a wing for a jet fighter, accuracy, efficiency, and safety must be sought beyond all else, in which case a more reliable but slower technique such as simulated annealing might be required.

SWARM INTELLIGENCE

Observe an ant colony up close and it may appear as if each ant is acting independently when performing such tasks as gathering food, removing debris from the nest, and fighting off predators. The same is true of bees in a hive, antelope in a herd, and even people hurriedly walking through a train station without bumping into one another. However, watch such groups more carefully, especially at a distance and over a long period of time, and collective behavior that appears as if it were centrally organized appears. If a bird attacks an ant nest, the ant colony jumps into action, with some ants carrying eggs deeper into the nest, others stinging the bird, and yet others repairing damage to the nest. The behavior of the colony may appear as if it were being carried out under the orders of an army general. For example, although one might expect to see all the ants run away or repel the invader, the colony instead somehow "knows" to divide itself into appropriately sized groups of protectors, soldiers, and repairers. Although the colony may appear as if it were following orders from a leader, it is not. Instead, such apparently guided behavior "emerges" from the interactions among individual ants. This kind of behavior, in which large numbers of individuals interact with one another to produce collective behavior that appears to be centrally organized, has come to be known by those in the field of artificial intelligence as "swarm intelligence."

The individuals in such systems typically follow only very simple rules and interact only with their neighbors (the individuals closest to them). Consider, for example, a flock of geese flying in a V-shaped formation. No single goose orders the others to arrange themselves in this shape. Instead, the V shape results from each individual goose following a few simple rules applied to its observations of the geese around it. In particular, each goose generally tries to fly forward. Second, each goose tries to align itself so that it is flying in the same direction as the geese around it. Third, each goose turns to avoid any other geese that are flying too close to it. Fourth, each goose tries to move closer toward other geese until it gets too close, in which case the third rule causes it to move farther away. Following these rules requires only that each bird be able to fly, control its own speed and direction of flight, and see the geese near it. Computer simulations confirm that a flock of geese that follows these simple rules will, in a relatively short time, collectively organize itself into a V shape, even though no one has instructed them to do so and even though no individual goose is trying to form such a shape. This is swarm intelligence at work. Amazingly, this formation is a highly efficient way for a flock of geese to fly, because it reduces the drag force experienced by each goose.

Swarm intelligence is of great interest to scientists and engineers because it demonstrates that complex behavior that seems to be guided by a centralized conscious intelligence can instead emerge from the interactions among individuals following only simple rules. Just picture how an entire school of fish darts away from an oncoming shark as soon as the shark comes within the vicinity of the "tail end" of the school. If the ways in which simple rules lead to seemingly intelligent behavior by groups could be understood, then people could develop artificially intelligent systems merely by creating simple rules for such systems to follow. In other words, artificial intelligence could be achieved without the need to understand and mimic all the complexities of human intelligence.

Computer scientists have made some progress in understanding swarm intelligence and incorporating it into computer systems. For example, swarm

`100111010010101010011001011101101010010101001`

Peter Bentley, Author and Expert on Biology-Inspired Computing

Dr. Peter Bentley, born in Colchester, England, in 1972, is a British computer scientist and an Honorary Senior Research Fellow at University College, London, where he runs the Digital Biology Interest Group. He earned a bachelor's degree in artificial intelligence from the University of Essex and a Ph.D. in evolutionary design from the University of Huddersfield at age 24. He is a respected authority in the field of evolutionary computation and digital biology as well as a popular writer and contributing editor to WIRED UK, a British version of the U.S. science and technology magazine.

Bentley's research focuses on *digital biology,* or complex systems such as artificial immune systems, computational development, *biomimicry* evolutionary algorithms,

(continues)

Peter Bentley, a leading computer scientist in the field of evolutionary computation and biology-inspired computing more generally, is shown here holding an autonomous bug-shaped robot that has a controller that was "evolved" by a genetic algorithm. The robot is able to navigate a maze and avoid obstacles using its evolved brain.   *(Dr. Peter J. Bentley)*

`100111010010101010011001011101101010010101001`

001101010010100111010110101010101011001010000 1

(continued)

and nanotechnology. He is fascinated by natural "emergent" processes, such as evolution, development, swarming systems, and the apparent resilience of these and other systems found in nature. He seeks to produce a self-assembling, self-adapting, self-designing, self-repairing device that would combine the complexity and adaptability of a living organism with computing power. Such a creation could be taught anything and become anything, unlimited in its applications. It could detect insurance fraud, write music, and even learn and predict human preferences. For example, Bentley "evolved" a beetle robot brain in an artificial environment where colliding with objects resulted in the death of the beetle. After a few hundred generations, the beetles that could not stop colliding with objects died, while the beetles that could continue to reproduce, resulting in a population of "intelligent" beetles that avoided collisions. His team is also working on "evolving" Formula 1 cars in ways that would increase their speed as well as self-building robots that are capable of evolving "cells" that can form structures and various shapes.

Dr. Bentley has written extensively about "digital biology" in both academic journals and popular science books in an effort to spread an understanding of biology-inspired computing to the general public.

001101010010100111010110101010101011001010000 1

intelligence has been used in feature films such as *Batman Returns* and *The Lord of the Rings* to simulate the movement of large crowds of simulated characters. Swarm intelligence has also been used to route packets in communications networks from one point to another and to fine-tune the parameters of artificial neural networks. Although this particular form of biology-inspired computing is still in its infancy, it holds much promise because it draws on the demonstrated ability of collections of organisms to coordinate their behavior in a wide variety of circumstances without the need to find, learn, and follow complex rules.

CONCLUSIONS

The wonders of the natural world continue to exceed the handiwork of humans. Plants and animals thrive in every existing environment, from the coldest mountaintops to the driest deserts to the scorching waters of undersea thermal vents. Certain plant seeds can remain viable for a hundred years, needing only a drop of water and sunlight to spring to life, while certain animals can regrow entire limbs lost to predators. Thousands of ants in a colony can coordinate their activities on the forest floor as if under the command of an army drill sergeant, while viruses can evolve to grow resistant to vaccines in just a few months. In comparison to such feats, human creations such as bridges and even computers seem to be the work of amateurs.

Such realizations are driving computer scientists to study the natural world for clues about how to improve both computer hardware and software. As they achieve some initial successes in developing artificial systems that can mimic the creative abilities of the human brain, the evolution of species by natural selection, and the healing powers of natural immune systems, computer scientists are learning other lessons as well. For example, engineers traditionally solve problems by starting from first principles and following well-accepted rules to produce results they can understand. Consider a civil engineer who designs a new bridge by starting from well-known principles of physics, following rules about bridge design (such as the proper materials to use in bridges of different sizes), to produce a design whose strengths and weaknesses can be predicted relatively accurately based on the engineer's understanding of mechanics.

In contrast, scientists who use biology-inspired computing often find themselves in the position of creating and setting up the initial conditions for an artificial biological system, such as an artificial neural network for controlling the flow of fluid through a waste treatment facility, and then letting that system run on its own and make its own decisions. The result—such as a decision by the neural network to temporarily stop the intake of water into the treatment plant at 2 P.M. on Sunday—might not be understood by the human who created the system and set it on its course. Furthermore, even though the human designer in some sense understands the process by which the system works, the system might independently develop new rules of operation that the human designer does not, and potentially cannot, understand. This puts people who create and use artificial biological systems in a very different position than that of traditional engineers.

One reason artificial biological systems can be difficult to understand is that, like the natural world, they can be sloppy, redundant, and inefficient. Just consider the human body, which has evolved over millions of years to include multiple redundant organs for performing the same function (such as the kidneys), organs that no longer perform any function (such as the appendix), and a variety of structural instabilities in the knees, spine, and hips that lead to frequent injuries, even when just performing everyday tasks. No human engineer would ever intentionally design a system having these features.

Yet such "flaws" can have corresponding benefits. What might at first glance appear to be an inefficient redundancy, such as the presence of two kidneys or a very large network of nerves, can be a significant benefit in the event that part of the body is injured. A human can lose one kidney and continue to live or have an entire region of nerves severed and continue to retain feeling in the rest of the body. In contrast, if the single central processing unit of a computer is damaged, the entire computer stops working. This is known as a "single point of failure," which is a dangerous feature for a living creature to have. Engineers are now learning this and attempt whenever possible to ensure that the artificial systems they create do not have single points of failure. The engineer's traditional single-minded focus on efficiency and elegance might have turned out to be a vice rather than a virtue.

Living things, whether plant or animal, also possess the ability to adapt to their environments throughout their lifetimes. Humans learn to avoid fire after touching it for the first time. Plants "learn" how to grow toward sunlight. Birds learn where to find the most food at different times during the year. In contrast, systems created using traditional human engineering typically remain fixed throughout their lifetimes. A bridge, once built, does not adapt to the world around it. Instead, it gradually crumbles and falls unless humans actively maintain it. Engineers are beginning to learn this lesson from the natural world and incorporate adaptability into artificial systems. Perhaps the simplest example comes in the form of today's personal computers, which automatically download and install security updates (known as "patches") onto themselves when they become available. The next step forward in this direction is "evolvable" computer hardware, which can effectively rewire itself on the fly to perform new functions in response to changing circumstances.

Although the artificial systems discussed in this chapter, such as artificial neural networks, evolutionary computation, and simulated annealing, were all originally designed based on knowledge gained from the real world of biology, now that such biology-inspired computing systems exist and have come to mirror their real-world counterparts increasingly accurately, studying the behavior of artificial biological systems can teach us about real-world biology. Studying the patterns in which artificial neurons fire can teach us about how neurons fire in a real brain. Observing population growth in simulated evolution can teach us about how different environmental conditions affect populations of various species in the natural world. Charting the course of a simulated ant colony can teach us about swarming behavior in real insects. Although care must be taken in drawing such conclusions because today's artificial biological systems lack the complexity of real-world biological systems, to the extent that we can draw any insights into the real world from the artificial world, we can feed that knowledge back into both natural biology and artificial biology (biology-inspired computing). The result is a positive feedback loop that can only improve the accuracy of the conclusions we draw in the future from both varieties of biology.

CHRONOLOGY

ca. 2700 B.C.E.	Egyptians introduce the first base 10 number system
ca. 2500 B.C.E.	Abacus mechanical calculating machine invented in Sumeria
ca. 300 B.C.E.	Greek mathematician Euclid proves theorems in geometry
179	*The Nine Chapters on the Mathematical Art* published during China's Han dynasty, including a mathematical proof of the Pythagorean theorem
ca. 500	Indian mathematician Aryabhata writes the *Aryabhatiya,* introducing the place-value number system for the first time
ca. 800	Arab mathematician Al-Kindi advances understanding of cryptography by inventing the frequency analysis technique for breaking certain kinds of substitution ciphers
904	Assyrian scientist Ibn Wahshiyya describes weather forecasting based on movement of winds in *Nabatean Agriculture*
ca. 1300	William of Ockham proposes the law of parsimony, later known as Occam's Razor, for selecting the simplest among competing hypotheses as the correct one
1623	Wilhelm Schickard invents first mechanical calculator
1643	Evangelista Torricelli invents the barometer for measuring atmospheric pressure
1645	Blaise Pascal invents Pascaline mechanical calculating machine
1783	Horace-Bénédict de Saussure designs the first hygrometer using a human hair to measure humidity

1805	Francis Beaufort creates the Beaufort scale for describing wind speed
1821	Charles Babbage invents the Difference Engine
1837	Charles Babbage first describes the Analytical Engine computing machine
1846	John Thomas Romney Robinson invents the cup anemometer for measuring wind speed
1884	Dorr Felt obtains a patent on the Comptometer mechanical calculator
1889	Herman Hollerith obtains a patent on a machine for automatically tabulating data stored on punch cards
1936	Alan Turing publishes "On Computable Numbers with an Application to the Entscheidungsproblem," introducing the concept of a general-purpose programming computer
1940	British government builds first Bombe device to crack the encryption code of the German Enigma encryption machine
1944	John von Neumann first describes the architecture of a stored-program computer in the "First Draft of a Report on the EDVAC"
	Howard Aiken ships the Harvard Mark I computer, the first large-scale automatic digital computer
1946	University of Pennsylvania unveils the ENIAC, the first general-purpose electronic computer
1949	An Wang and Way-Dong Woo create the first computer magnetic core memory
1951	Marvin Minsky creates the first artificial neural network
1952	Ray Bradbury introduces concept of the "butterfly effect" in a short story entitled "A Sound of Thunder"

1960	First weather satellite launched, giving meteorologists a view of the entire planet
1961	Jay Forrester publishes *Industrial Dynamics,* the first book on system dynamics
1963	Ivan Sutherland designs Sketchpad, arguably the first CAD software
1964	Lawrence J. Fogel introduces the concept of evolutionary computation in his dissertation, "On the Organization of Intellect"
1971	Intel releases the 4004 central processing unit (CPU), the first complete CPU on a single chip
1976	Kenneth Appel and Wolfgang Haken use a computer to solve the four-color theorem
1977	Ron Rivest, Adi Shamir, and Leonard Adleman develop the RSA encryption algorithm
1978	First version of flight simulator software offered for home computers by subLOGIC Corporation
1983	Stephen Wiesner publishes a paper entitled "Conjugate Code," which introduces the concept of quantum cryptography, a type of cryptography based on quantum systems
1994	Leonard Adleman first describes DNA computing in "Molecular Computation of Solutions to Combinatorial Problems"
1995	Andrew Wiles proves Fermat's last theorem
1999	Transport Security Layer, an Internet encryption protocol, first defined
2001	IBM launches Autonomic Computing initiative
2003	Linden Lab launches Second Life virtual world
2005	The BioBricks Foundation, a nonprofit that supports the development and responsible use of standard DNA parts, is founded

2007	Gross domestic product of Second Life virtual economy exceeds $200 million
2008	John Harrison formalizes a proof of the prime number theorem (PNT) using a computer software proof system he authored called HOL (Higher Order Logic) Light
	Laerdal Medical introduces SimMan 3G, a sophisticated medical training mannequin that can simulate a wide variety of health conditions and react to the administration of medications and procedures
2009	Dr. David Clarke performs the first virtual reality surgical procedure using data modeled on a real patient; he then removed the patient's benign brain tumor 24 hours after performing the virtual surgery
2010	A team of researchers at the University of Toronto shows that a quantum cryptography key that was previously thought to be secure could be hacked
	Linden Lab announces a new direction for Second Life that focuses on providing a Web browser interface and eliminates the need for software downloads; 30 percent of Linden Lab's employees are laid off as part of the company's new strategy
	The European Space Agency initiates Mars500, the first simulated space flight to Mars
	NASA opens its Center for Climate Simulation, where supercomputing, sophisticated data modeling, and computer graphics will be used for advanced research in weather and climate prediction
	The U.S. Department of Energy signs a $47-million contract with supercomputer manufacturer Cray, Inc., to provide a next-generation supercomputer for climate research and modeling

DNA-based logic gates capable of carrying out calculations within the human body are constructed by researchers at the Hebrew University of Jerusalem in Israel

Space flight engineers at Colorado State University use genetic programming to find a way to double the life expectancy of electrostatic ion engines used on space missions

2011   Digital forensics toolmaker Elcomsoft cracks the data security scheme on Apple's iPhone 4 smartphone; makes tool for cracking iPhone 4 encryption available to law enforcement agencies, intelligence agencies, and professional forensic investigators

Google releases a security patch for its Android phones that fixes a vulnerability reported to have affected 99 percent of Android users, through which hackers could access personal data on Android phones wirelessly

Scientists at the Max Planck Institute of Biology and the University of Illinois build a computer model the bacteria *E. coli* that responds to sugar in its environment and accurately simulates the behavior of living cells

Federal Aviation Administration revises its training rules to include a greater emphasis on using full-motion flight simulators to train crews to work together when handling rare real-world flight emergencies that have led to fatal crashes in recent years, such as stalling of airplane engines

Excalibur Publishing releases Surgery Simulator, which allows personal computer users to perform simulated surgeries on cataracts, varicose veins, gall bladders, and tonsils, among others

A coalition of scientists from eight nations begins collaborating to develop climate simulation software that will be able to leverage the next generation of supercomputers to run climate simulations at scales that are 1,000 times larger than those possible today

Researchers at the University of Texas at Austin use an artificial neural network to simulate a human brain that releases excess dopamine and find that the simulated brain exhibits symptoms of schizophrenia

Jian-Jun Shu, a professor of mechanical and aerospace engineering at the Nanyang Technical University in Singapore, uses DNA to perform the arithmetic operations of addition and division

Professor Frank Neumann of the University of Adelaide uses evolutionary algorithms to select the optimal placement of up to 1,000 wind turbines to maximize the energy they produce

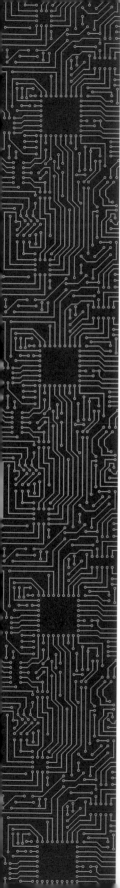

GLOSSARY

abacus an ancient mechanical device for performing arithmetic by rearranging beads on pegs

Analytical Engine a computer invented in the 19th century by Charles Babbage, which was capable of being programmed to perform various calculations automatically

anemometer a device for measuring wind speed; used in forecasting weather

arithmetic logic unit (ALU) the part of a computer's CPU that performs addition, subtraction, multiplication, and division

artificial immune system a computational system, usually implemented in software, that mimics how the immune systems of living organisms work in order to enable computers to solve problems and avoid failures

artificial neural network software that mimics how the neurons in the human brain interact with one another; often used to recognize patterns in large amounts of data

autonomic computing system a computer system that manages itself to perform functions such as fixing bugs and avoiding crashes in the face of changes to its environment

avatar a graphical representation of a computer user, often used in a videogame or virtual world; a person's avatar may or may not resemble the person's appearance in the real world

axiom a statement assumed, but not proven, to be true in a mathematical system, such as the axiom in Euclidean geometry that the shortest distance between two points in a plane is a straight line

barometer a device that measures air pressure for purposes of predicting the weather

Beaufort scale a system for describing wind speed, created by Francis Beaufort

binary numbers   numbers written using the base 2 numeral system, which employs only the digits 0 and 1; widely used in computer technology because they can be represented by devices, such as transistors, that have only two states, such as "on" and "off"

bioinformatics   the use of mathematics and computers to study biological systems

biomimicry   computers and other systems designed to incorporate features from nature

Bombe (decryption device)   an electromechanical decryption machine designed by computer pioneers Alan Turing and Gordon Welchman in 1939; used to decrypt messages encoded by the German Enigma machine

butterfly effect   the idea that a butterfly flapping its wings may change weather conditions elsewhere in the world; although not technically accurate, reflects the more technical notion of "sensitive dependence on initial conditions"

calculator   a device, usually containing mechanical and/or electrical components, that performs calculations

central processing unit (CPU)   the electronic circuitry at the heart of a computer that performs computations

chip   another name for an **integrated circuit**

ciphertext   a message in encrypted form such that it cannot be read without first decrypting it using an appropriate key

climate modeling   systems of mathematical equations based on the laws of physics, fluid dynamics, and chemistry that are used to understand and predict Earth's climate

complex systems   systems, such as the weather and stock markets, whose behavior is too complex to predict based merely on studying individual parts of the system

computer-aided design (CAD) software   a type of software that can be used to create 2-D and 3-D models of physical products

computer-assisted proof a mathematical proof generated using computer software

cryptographic key data that may be used to encrypt and/or decrypt a message; examples are **private keys** and **public keys**

cuneiform a Sumerian writing system that originated around 3400 B.C.E.

cryptography the study of **encryption** and **decryption**

decimal numbers numbers written using the base 10 numeral system, in which each position indicates a power of 10; may also refer to numbers that use a decimal point to represent a fractional value

decryption descrambling a scrambled message to reveal the original, unscrambled message

digit a number from 0 through 9; also refers to fingers on the human hand, which were used to count before written number systems and mechanical calculating devices existed

digital biology a variety of fields of computer science in which knowledge gained from biology is used to design computer systems to work like biological systems

digital certificate an electronic document that uses a digital signature to associate a **public key** with a person's identity, such as the person's name, organization, and address, for the purpose of verifying that the public key belongs to the person

digital signature electronic data that can be attached to a message to indicate that a particular person has signed the message; a secure digital signature is very difficult to forge

DNA computing manipulating DNA to perform computations

EDVAC (Electronic Discrete Variable Automatic Computer) an electronic computer built in 1949; had a binary architecture and was the first general-purpose computer that used a stored program

electronic calculator a device that performs mathematical calculations using electronic circuitry

encryption   scrambling a message so that it cannot be understood without first descrambling it (see **decryption**); often used to keep messages hidden from spies

ENIAC (Electronic Numerical Integrator and Computer)   the first electronic general-purpose computer; built in 1946, the ENIAC had a decimal architecture and could be reprogrammed to solve a variety of problems

evolutionary computation   a field of computer science that develops software that solves problems by mimicking how organisms evolve to fit in their natural environments

flight simulator   computer software and/or hardware that simulates the flight of an airplane using three-dimensional animation, sound, and sometimes physical movement and feedback

floating point representation   a digital format for storing numbers very precisely

FLOPS (floating point operations per second)   a measure of how quickly a computer can perform calculations

four-color theorem   a mathematical theorem that states that any map can be colored by no more than four colors without the same color touching itself, eventually proved with the assistance of computer software (see **theorem prover**)

general-purpose programmable computer   a computer that can be programmed to run an infinite variety of software

Harvard Mark I computer   the first large-scale automatic digital computer, developed by IBM in 1944 for Harvard University

Hollerith tabulator   an electrical tabulation machine designed in 1890 by the American inventor Herman Hollerith for use in the 1890 U.S. Census

hygrometer   an instrument to measure the humidity of air, first described by Nicholas Cusa in the 15th century

integrated circuit (IC)   a set of electronic miniaturized components and connectors that are etched on the surface of a semiconductor chip; used in a wide variety of electronic devices, from cell phones to computers

lemma   a statement proven as true as a stepping stone to proving a mathematical theorem

math coprocessor   computer circuitry designed to perform mathematical calculations very quickly

mathematical notation   the system of symbols used to represent mathematical objects and ideas, including numerals, letters, special symbols (e.g., +, −, =) and other more complex representations

mathematical proof   a formal demonstration that a mathematical statement is true

mechanical calculator   a device that performs mathematical calculations without using electricity, usually via a combination of gears and levers

memory   the circuitry in a computer that stores software and data

microprocessor   an **integrated circuit** that incorporates the functions of a computer **central processing unit** (CPU) on a single microchip

modeling   the process of creating a simplified physical or virtual representation of a system, such as the weather, in order to learn about the system without having to study it directly

parallel processing   using two or more computer processors in conjunction to perform computations more quickly

Pascaline   a mechanical calculating device invented by the French mathematician Blaise Pascal around 1650

physics engine   the component in a simulator that mimics the natural laws of physics and thereby enables the simulator to accurately depict the motion of objects and their interactions with each other

pictograph   pictures used by ancient Egyptians to represent numbers

plaintext   an unencrypted message that can easily be read, such as a message written in plain English

printed circuit board (PCB)   a thin plate on which electronic components are installed and connected with etched conductive pathways

private key   a **cryptographic key** a person keeps secret for the purpose of decrypting messages encrypted using that person's **public key**

processor   the component of a computer that reads instructions from **memory** and carries them out

public key   a **cryptographic key** a person may publish for others to use to encrypt messages addressed to that person; knowledge of a person's public key does not enable one to decrypt messages addressed to that person

public-key encryption   a kind of **encryption** that allows Person A to publish his or her **public key** so that other people can use that key to encrypt messages to send to Person A, such that only Person A can decrypt those messages (using Person A's **private key**)

punch card   a paper card in which holes are punched to represent numbers or instructions; early computers received information on punch cards instead of tape or disk

Roman numerals   a number system used in ancient Rome based on letters of the Roman alphabet, such as I, V, X, L, and M; arithmetic is difficult to perform using Roman numerals

RSA encryption algorithm   a famous public key encryption algorithm used to encrypt communications on the Internet and to create digital signatures

scytale   a device used by the ancient Greeks to send encrypted messages

shared-key encryption   a system for transmitting encrypted messages in which both the sender and recipient must have the same encryption key

simulated annealing   a technique for solving problems in a way that mimics how annealing of atoms occurs in metals; usually implemented in software to solve problems that are difficult to solve using traditional software algorithms

simulator   software that mimics the real world, such as a flight simulator that mimics an airplane in flight

slide rule   a mechanical device that scientists and engineers used to perform calculations by hand before electronic calculators and computers were invented

swarm intelligence   a type of artificial intelligence that solves problems using the collective behavior of decentralized, self-organized systems; inspired by the ways in which swarms of ants and other insects behave

theorem   a mathematical statement that has been proven to be true using a **mathematical proof**

theorem prover   software that attempts to prove whether mathematical theorems are correct

traveling salesman problem   a well-known computing problem that involves finding a path from one place to another, passing through a predetermined number of points only once and using a given set of one-way paths

TSL (transport security layer, formerly known as secure sockets layer)   a form of encryption frequently used on the Internet

universal machine   another name for a **general-purpose programmable computer**

vacuum tube   the primary computing component in early electrical computers, eventually replaced by the transistor

virtual world   a world simulated by software, usually displayed using animated three-dimensional graphics and used for social interactions, commerce, or entertainment

von Neumann architecture   a design for a computer in which a program's instructions and data are stored in a single memory; named after the computer pioneer John von Neumann

weather modeling   the creation of a simplified model of weather patterns, usually using a computer, to enable storms and other weather events to be predicted

FURTHER RESOURCES

The following resources are arranged according to chapter title.

"Before Computers"

BOOKS

Babbage, Charles. *Passages from the Life of a Philosopher.* Surrey, U.K.: Merchant Books, 2008. A collection of Babbage's works, including autobiographical notes as well as his writings on the Analytical Engine and the notes by Lady Lovelace.

Eames, Charles, and Ray Eames. *A Computer Perspective.* Cambridge, Mass.: Harvard University Press, 1990. A graphic anthology on the origins and history of the computer through 1950, designed to be used as a quick reference.

Goldstine, Herman H. *The Computer from Pascal to von Neumann.* Princeton, N.J.: Princeton University Press, 1972. A history of computer development from Pascal through the end of World War II, written by a computer scientist who was part of the team that developed the ENIAC computer. Goldstine was also a colleague of the renowned computer pioneer John von Neumann.

Ifrah, Georges. *The Universal History of Computing: From the Abacus to the Quantum Computer.* Hoboken, N.J.: Wiley & Sons, 2000. The highly acclaimed author and mathematician Georges Ifrah describes the history of computers, beginning with the development of number systems through early calculating machines and the development of modern computers.

McLeish, John. *The Story of Numbers: How Mathematics Has Shaped Civilization.* New York: Ballantine Books, 1994. An exploration of the history of mathematics, tracing the rise of various number systems from ancient times up until the modern computer era.

Swade, Doron. *The Difference Engine: Charles Babbage and the Quest to Build the First Computer.* London: Little, Brown, 2001. Written by the assistant director at the London Museum of Science who led the team that built the Difference Engine, the book examines both the difficulties encountered by Babbage and the process of how the engine was built by the London Museum.

Swedin, Eric G., and David L. Ferro. *Computers: The Life Story of a Technology.* Baltimore: Johns Hopkins University Press, 2007. A short history of computer technology from ancient times to the modern day and an examination of the ways in which the computer has become a standard fixture of everyday life.

ARTICLES

"IBM's ASCC Introduction (a.k.a. The Harvard Mark I)." IBM Archives Web site. Available online. URL: http://www-03.ibm.com/ibm/history/exhibits/markI/markI_intro.html. Accessed January 5, 2011. Provides details about the Harvard Mark I, the first large-scale automatic digital calculator.

"Turing Machines." *Stanford Encyclopedia of Philosophy.* Available online. URL: http://plato.stanford.edu/entries/turing-machine. Accessed February 4, 2011. Describes the abstract computational devices known as Turing machines. Named for the computer science pioneer Alan Turing, the concept is used to investigate the limits of computability.

WEB SITES

Abacus. Available online. URL: http://www.ee.ryerson.ca/~elf/abacus/index.html. Accessed February 4, 2011. Award-winning Web site dedicated to the history and modern use of the abacus counting device. Includes an interactive abacus tutorial.

The Antikythera Mechanism Research Project. Available online. URL: http://www.antikythera-mechanism.gr. Accessed February 4, 2011. Web site for the international collaborative project researching the function and significance of the Antikythera mechanism, considered by scientists to be one of the most important archaeological artifacts ever discovered.

The Babbage Engine. Available online. URL: http://www.computerhistory.org/babbage. Accessed February 4, 2011. Web site that covers the history and operating principles of Babbage's Difference and Analytical Engines. Hosted by the Computer History Museum in San Jose, California.

John W. Mauchly and the Development of the ENIAC Computer. Available online. URL: http://www.library.upenn.edu/exhibits/rbm/mauchly/jwmintro.html. Accessed February 4, 2011. University of Pennsylvania online exhibition on the emergence of modern computing and the contributions of John W. Mauchly, who worked with J. Presper Eckert on the design of the ENIAC and EDVAC computers.

Pascaline. Available online. URL: http://www.thocp.net/hardware/pascaline. htm. Accessed February 4, 2011. Information about Blaise Pascal and his Pascaline calculator on a Web site dedicated to the history of computers.

"Cryptography"

BOOKS

Bauer, F. L. *Decrypted Secrets: Methods and Maxims of Cryptography.* New York: Springer, 1996. A classic reference work on cryptology, covering both secret codes and their uses (cryptology) and the process of decrypting codes (cryptanalysis). The inclusion of exciting and amusing stories from the history of cryptology makes this book interesting for a wide range of readers.

Singh, Simon. *The Code Book: The Science of Secrecy from Ancient Egypt to Quantum Cryptography.* New York: Anchor, 2000. An excellent primer on cryptography, exploring the impact on culture and society of the creation and cracking of coded messages.

Wobst, Reinhard. *Cryptology Unlocked.* Translated by Angelica Shafir. Hoboken, N.J.: John Wiley & Sons, 2007. A nonmathematical introduction to cryptography, encryption, and cryptanalysis.

Wrixon, Fred B. *Codes, Ciphers, Secrets and Cryptic Communication: Making and Breaking Secret Messages from Hieroglyphs to the Internet.* London: Black Dog & Leventhal, 2005. The world history of secret communication, written by an expert in codes, military history, and espionage.

ARTICLES

"Solving the Enigma: History of the Cryptanalytic Bombe." National Security Agency pamphlet. Available online. URL: http://ed-thelen.org/comp-hist/ NSA-Enigma.html. Accessed February 4, 2011. A history of the Enigma and Bombe cryptanalytic devices used during World War II.

WEB SITES

Cryptographic Software Solutions and How to Use Them. Available online. URL: http://www.seifried.org/security/cryptography/crypto-book/index

.html. Accessed February 4, 2011. An online primer on cryptography by the security analyst Kurt Seifried.

How PGP Works. Available online. URL: http://www.pgpi.org/doc/pgpintro. Accessed February 4, 2011. A description of how PGP encryption works. PGP (Pretty Good Privacy) is commonly used for encrypting and decrypting e-mail messages.

"Mathematical Proofs"

BOOKS

Cupillari, Antonella. *The Nuts and Bolts of Proofs.* Burlington, Mass.: Academic Press, 2005. A simple and popular guidebook for reading, understanding, and constructing proofs.

Grattan-Guinness, Ivor. *The Norton History of the Mathematical Sciences: The Rainbow of Mathematics.* New York: W.W. Norton & Co., 1998. A history of mathematics, with an emphasis on concepts and on the relations of mathematical innovations to other scientific discoveries.

Mason, J., L. Burton, and K. Stacey. *Thinking Mathematically.* London: Addison Wesley, 1982. An exploration into the processes that characterize mathematical thinking. A useful aid for students of higher mathematics.

Velleman, Daniel J. *How to Prove It: A Structured Approach.* Cambridge: Cambridge University Press, 2006. An introduction to mathematical proofs, including a step-by-step breakdown of the techniques used in constructing proofs.

Wilson, Robin. *Four Colors Suffice: How the Map Problem Was Solved.* London: Penguin Books, 2002. An easy-to-read history of how the four color theorem was proven, written in an accessible form for the general reader.

WEB SITES

The Four Color Theorem. Available online. URL: http://people.math.gatech. edu/~thomas/FC/fourcolor.html. Accessed February 4, 2011. Provides details about the 1997 proof of the famous four color theorem devised by Neil Robertson, Daniel P. Sanders, Paul Seymour, and Robin Thomas based on the Appel-Haken proof of 1976. Includes a brief history of earlier proofs of the theorem.

Notices of the American Mathematical Society. Available online. URL: http://www.ams.org/notices/200811/index.html. Accessed February 4,

2011. A special issue of this online academic journal from December 2008 devoted to articles on computer-assisted proofs.

Proof. Available online. URL: http://www.jimloy.com/math/proof.htm. Accessed February 4, 2011. Descriptions and examples of a wide variety of mathematical proofs.

Proofs in Mathematics. Available online. URL: http://www.cut-the-knot.org/ proofs/index.shtml. Accessed February 4, 2011. Cut-the-Knot is a popular educational Web site that includes dozens of examples of famous proofs, invalid proofs, and fallacies.

Types of Proof. Available online. URL: http://www.math.csusb.edu/notes/ proofs/pfnot/node4.html. Accessed February 4, 2011. Mathematical proof tutorial hosted by California State University at San Bernardino.

"Simulation"

BOOKS

Aldrich, Clark. *Learning by Doing.* San Francisco: Pfeiffer, 2005. A comprehensive explanation of how educational simulations are researched, constructed, and marketed. The book covers all types of simulators, from low-tech to the most complex computer games and flight simulators.

————. *Simulations and the Future of Learning.* San Francisco: Pfeiffer, 2003. Aldrich provides details on the life cycle of a modern computer simulation based on his experiences as a leading designer of simulations.

Bonk, Curtis J. *The World Is Open: How Web Technology Is Revolutionizing Education.* San Francisco: Jossey-Bass, 2009. An examination of technological trends that will have an impact on education in the 21st century, including ebooks, open source software, and electronic collaboration.

White, Brian A. *Second Life: A Guide to Your Virtual World.* Indianapolis: Que, 2007. This guide to the virtual world of Second Life includes interviews with residents, tips for getting started, and explanations of advanced techniques for creating a virtual life.

ARTICLES

Glaser, Mark. "Your Guide to Virtual Worlds." PBS Web Site. (October 10, 2007) Available online. URL: http://www.pbs.org/mediashift/2007/10/ your-guide-to-virtual-worlds283.html. Accessed February 4, 2011. An overview of virtual worlds, including a history, glossary, and list of virtual world Web sites.

Hirz, Mario. "Advanced 3D-CAD Design Methods in Education and Research." Institute of Automotive Engineering, Graz University of Technology, Austria. URL: http://www.iiisci.org/journal/CV$/sci/pdfs/GF680NA.pdf. Accessed February 4, 2011. An examination of how 3-D CAD supports simulation procedures for automotive design, including vehicle safety testing and feasibility studies.

WEB SITES

The Best CAD Software History on the Web. Available online. URL: http://www.cadazz.com. Accessed February 4, 2011. A comprehensive history of CAD software, beginning with Ivan Sutherland's groundbreaking Sketchpad system in the early 1960s and ending with "virtual product development" of the 2000s.

A Brief History of Aircraft Flight Simulation. Available online. URL: http://homepage.ntlworld.com/bleep/SimHist1.html. Accessed February 4, 2011. A detailed history of flight simulators, beginning with training devices from the early 20th century. The Web site includes drawings and photos.

Flight Simulator History. Available online. URL: http://fshistory.simflight.com/fsh/index.htm. Accessed February 4, 2011. The history of Microsoft's Flight Simulator software and information about Bruce Artwick, its creator.

Industrial Design and Styling. Available online. URL: http://www.plm.automation.siemens.com/en_sg/products/nx/design/industrial/index.shtml. Accessed February 4, 2011. Web page for NX CAD system with link to demo showing how rapid prototyping allows industrial designers to make changes in the design of a product and immediately see a 3-D simulation of the finished product.

Introducing Virtual Environments. Available online. URL: http://archive.ncsa.illinois.edu/Cyberia/VETopLevels/VR.Overview.html#toc. Accessed February 4, 2011. Web site hosted by the University of Illinois that explores the history, technology, applications, and future of virtual reality.

"Weather"

BOOKS

Aczel, Amir D. *The Riddle of the Compass: The Invention That Changed the World.* New York: Harvest Books, 2002. A history of the development of the compass, from 11th-century China to 14th-century Italy.

Burroughs, William J., Bob Crowder, Ted Robertson, Eleanor Vallier-Talbot, and Richard Whitaker. *Weather, a Nature Company Guide.* New York: Time-Life Books, 1996. Photos and text explaining all types of weather and the history of weather forecasting.

Geiger, Peter, and Sondra Duncan. *Farmers' Almanac 2010.* Lewiston, Maine: Geiger, 2009. Published annually since 1818, this almanac includes long-term weather forecasts along with astronomical data, gardening and household tips, fishing advice, and articles on a variety of other topics. URL: http://www.farmersalmanac.com.

Huer, Scott. *Defining the Wind: The Beaufort Scale and How a 19th-Century Admiral Turned Science into Poetry.* New York: Three Rivers Press, 2005. A book that combines a look at the life of Admiral Beaufort and the history of defining the wind and weather.

Lockhart, Gary. *The Weather Companion: An Album of Meteorological History, Science, and Folklore.* New York: Wiley & Sons, 1988. A compendium of meteorological facts and mythology designed for readers who are beginning to explore the subject of weather.

Monmonier, Mark. *Air Apparent: How Meteorologists Learned to Map, Predict, and Dramatize Weather.* Chicago: University of Chicago Press, 1999. Meteorology is explained through a description of the history of weather maps.

ARTICLES

Gutro, Rob. "What's the Difference Between Weather and Climate?" NASA Web Site. (February 1, 2005) Available online. URL: http://www.nasa.gov/mission_pages/noaa-n/climate/climate_weather.html. Accessed February 4, 2011. Discusses the differences between daily weather changes and long-term climate patterns and the importance of climate research.

WEB SITES

The History of Numerical Weather Prediction. NOAA (National Oceanic and Atmospheric Administration) Web site. Available online. URL: http://celebrating200years.noaa.gov/foundations/numerical_wx_pred/welcome.html#intro. Accessed February 4, 2011. A history of the use of mathematical models and computers for weather prediction.

Transforming the Weather Business. NOAA (National Oceanic and Atmospheric Administration) Web site. Available online. URL: http://celebrating200years.noaa.gov/transformations/weather/welcome.html. Accessed February 4, 2011. Describes how the business of weather forecasting has been transformed and improved by technology.

Weather Forecasting Through the Ages. NASA Earth Observatory Web site. Available online. URL: http://earthobservatory.nasa.gov/Features/WxForecasting/wx.php. Accessed February 4, 2011. A comprehensive history of weather forecasting, from ancient times to the modern day.

"Computer-Inspired Biology"

BOOKS

Amos, Martyn. *Genesis Machines: The New Science of Biocomputing.* New York: Overlook Hardcover, 2008. A survey of the field of biocomputing and a look into its future. Amos was awarded the first Ph.D. in DNA computing.

———. *Theoretical and Experimental DNA Computation.* New York: Springer, 2005. An overview of DNA computing, beginning with Leonard Adleman's initial experiment. All major theoretical models are described, along with possible future developments.

Maddox, Brenda. *Rosalind Franklin: The Dark Lady of DNA.* New York: Harper Perennial, 2003. A biography of Rosalind Franklin, the mostly unknown scientist whose research contributed to the discovery of the structure of DNA.

ARTICLES

Adleman, Leonard. "Computing with DNA." *Scientific American.* (August 1998): 54–61. Available online. URL: http://www.cs.virginia.edu/~robins/Computing_with_DNA.pdf. Accessed November 8, 2010. Adleman's description and explanation of his groundbreaking proof-of-concept use of DNA to solve the Hamilton path (Traveling Salesman) problem.

Ganapati, Priya. "DNA May Help Build the Next Generation of Chips." *Wired Gadget Lab* (August 17, 2009). Available online. URL: http://www.wired.com/gadgetlab/2009/08/dna-chips. Accessed February 4, 2011. Describes current research into DNA computing at some of the top labs in the nation.

WEB SITES

DNA History. University of Delaware Web site. Available online. URL: http://www.ceoe.udel.edu/extreme2004/genomics/dnahistory.html. Accessed February 4, 2011. A history of the discovery of the structure of DNA by Nobel Prize–winning scientists James Watson and Francis Crick.

The New Genetics. National Institute of General Medical Sciences Web site. Available online. URL: http://publications.nigms.nih.gov/thenewgenetics/index.html. Accessed February 4, 2011. An overview of DNA and genetics, including a look at the future convergence of biology and computer science and the increasingly important role of genetics in modern society.

What Is DNA? United States National Library of Medicine Genetics Home Reference Web site. Available online. URL: http://ghr.nlm.nih.gov/handbook/basics/dna. Accessed February 4, 2011. Basic information about DNA, genes, and chromosomes.

What Is DNA Computing? RSA Laboratories Web site. Available online. URL: http://www.rsa.com/rsalabs/node.asp?id=2355. Accessed February 4, 2011. A description of the theory of DNA computing and its relation to cryptography.

"Biology-Inspired Computing"

BOOKS

Bentley, Peter J. *Digital Biology: How Nature Is Transforming Our Technology and Our Lives*. New York: Simon & Schuster, 2007. A description of how computer scientists are attempting to create digital universes that reflect the natural world.

———. *Evolutionary Design by Computers*. San Francisco: Morgan Kaufman, 1999. A collection of essays on recent research in evolutionary computing.

Forbes, Nancy. *Imitation of Life: How Biology Is Inspiring Computing.* Cambridge, Mass.: The MIT Press, 2005. A survey of developments that led to attempts to incorporate biological processes into computing and a guide to current research.

Sipper, Moshe. *Machine Nature: The Coming Age of Bio-Inspired Computing.* New York: McGraw-Hill, 2002. A compelling look at current advances in robots and computers, with an emphasis on nature-inspired technology such as neural networks and evolutionary algorithms.

WEB SITES

Biomimicry Institute. Available online. URL: http://www.biomimicry institute.org/about-us. Accessed February 4, 2011. Web site for a research institute dedicated to the new discipline of biomimicry, which uses designs and processes found in nature to solve human problems. An example of biomimicry is designing a solar cell based on the structure of a leaf.

Digital Biology. Available online. URL: http://www.digitalbiology.com. Accessed February 4, 2011. Web site dedicated to a propriety computer software system that combines computer animation and artificial life research to produce interactive simulations of various life forms.

Evolutionary Algorithms. Sandia Labs Web site. Available online. URL: http://www.cs.sandia.gov/opt/survey/ea.html. Accessed February 4, 2011. A description of genetic algorithms and programming and evolutionary programming concepts.

Neural Networks. Imperial College London Web site. Available online. URL: http://www.doc.ic.ac.uk/~nd/surprise_96/journal/vol4/cs11/report.html. Accessed February 4, 2011. An introduction to artificial neural networks and their applications.

Swarm Intelligence. Carleton College Canada Web site. Available online. URL: http://www.sce.carleton.ca/netmanage/tony/swarm.html. Accessed February 4, 2011. Links to slide shows, presentations, research papers, and simulation software related to the concept of swarm intelligence.

INDEX

Italic page numbers indicate illustrations.